Illustrators 22

THE TWENTY SECOND
ANNUAL EXHIBITION OF ILLUSTRATION
HELD IN THE GALLERIES OF THE
SOCIETY OF ILLUSTRATORS
128 EAST 63RD STREET, NEW YORK
FEBRUARY 6 THROUGH APRIL 10, 1980

International Distributors
CANADA: Saunders of Toronto, Ltd., Don Mills, Ontario.
FRANCE: Graphis Distribution, Milon-La-Chapelle, F-78470 St.-Remy-Les Chevreuse.
SWITZERLAND, FEDERAL REPUBLIC OF GERMANY AND AUSTRIA: Arthur Niggli, Ltd., Publishers,
    CH-9052 Niederteufen, Switzerland.
UNITED KINGDOM: Transatlantic Book Service Ltd., 24 Red Lion Street, London WCIR 4 PX,
    England.
OTHER EUROPEAN COUNTRIES: Fleetbooks, c/o Feffer & Simons, B.V. Rijnkade 170, P.O. Box 112,
    1382 GT Weesp, Netherlands.
REST OF WORLD: Fleetbooks, c/o Feffer & Simons, Inc., 100 Park Avenue, New York, N.Y. 10017.

FORBES LLOYD LINKHORN, *Editor*   **ROBERT HALLOCK,** *Designer*

THE TWENTY SECOND ANNUAL OF AMERICAN ILLUSTRATION

Published for the Society of Illustrators by **HASTINGS HOUSE, PUBLISHERS, INC.,** New York 10016

HALL OF FAME
⇛ 1958-1980 ⇜

1958   Norman Rockwell

1959   Dean Cornwell

ILLUSTRATORS 22 JURORS

ADVERTISING
Jerry Pinkney, *Chairman*
Birney Lettick
William K. Plummer
Alan Reingold
John Schoenherr
Catherine Siracusa
William Teason
John Witt

EDITORIAL
Jim Sharpe, *Chairman*
Mike Eagle
Gordon Fisher
Charles Gehm
Neil Hardy
Sunday Hendrickson
Stan Hunter
Stan Mack
George Stavrinos

BOOK
Warren Rogers, *Chairman*
Ed Brodkin
George Jones
Roger Kastel
Rick MacDonald
Bob Pepper
Howard Rogers
Charles Santore
Don Stivers

INSTITUTIONAL
Alan E. Cober, *Chairman*
Harvey Dinnerstein
Gerry Gersten
Bob Giusti
Gordon Johnson
Peter Kleinman
Alan Magee
Marie Michal
Bob Ziering

TV/FILM
Tracy Sugarman, *Chairman*
Joan Hall
Saul Mandel
Jessica Weber

1959   Harold Von Schmidt   1960   Fred G. Cooper   1961   Floyd Davis

Illustrators 22

THE SOCIETY OF ILLUSTRATORS

OFFICERS (1979-80)

Honorary President . . . . Harold Von Schmidt
President . . . . Warren Rogers
Executive Vice President . . . . John Witt
Vice President . . . . Art Weithas
Treasurer . . . . Walter Hortens
Associate Treasurer . . . . Diane Dillon
Secretary . . . . Miriam Schottland
House Chairman . . . . Gerald McConnell

ILLUSTRATORS 22 COMMITTEE

Show Chairman . . . . Sandy Huffaker
Annual Book Editor . . . . Forbes Lloyd Linkhorn
Annual Book Designer . . . . Robert Hallock
Poster Artist . . . . Daniel Schwartz
Poster Designer . . . . Walter Bernard
Hanging Chairman . . . . Doug Cramer
Executive Director . . . . Arpi Ermoyan
Show Coordinator . . . . Terry Brown
Show Staff . . . . Jill Bossert
                                                          Cathy Citarella
                                                          Anna Lee Fuchs
                                                          Norma Pimsler

1962   Edward A. Wilson   1963   Walter Biggs   1964   Arthur William Brown

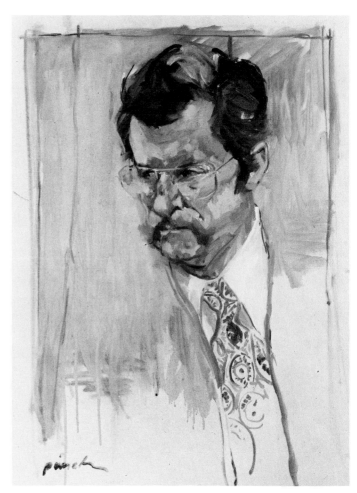

ALVIN J. PIMSLER

PRESIDENT'S MESSAGE by Warren Rogers

I was in my studio the other night looking at Illustrators '59, the first Annual of American Illustration published by the Society of Illustrators, and what a collection of famous (and later to be famous) names!

22 years later we're looking at Illustrators 22 (1981) and I'm equally impressed by the work. The quality never seems to change, just some of the names.

The Illustrators Annual, whatever the number, is by anyone's standard *the* record of the very best illustration for its given year, and this year's issue, 22, is no exception!

My congratulations to all of you whose art appears in these pages. You're obviously the famous (or soon to be famous) illustrators of this year.

1965   Al Parker

1966   Al Dorne

1967   Robert Fawcett

SHOW CHAIRMAN'S MESSAGE by Sandy Huffaker

As an artist, I have always submitted only my best pieces of art done during the year to the Society of Illustrators Annual Exhibition. As Chairman of *Illustrators 22*, it was my privilege to see the thousands of entries from all over the world, and finding weak work was rare indeed. Our juries had the even harder task of picking the best selections that appear in this book. Fresh approaches by established artists were honored, but unheralded newcomers also made a splash, with one new midwestern artist having five paintings (the SI limit) selected.

After seeing first-hand all the hundreds of details involved in putting this exhibition together, special thanks has to go to Arpi Ermoyan, Terry Brown and the staff for somehow making it all happen year after year.

EDITOR'S COMMENT by Forbes Lloyd Linkhorn

'Twas only yesterday, it seems, when I had the honor of editing another Annual for the Society of Illustrators, but that was, in fact, nearly ten years ago. Each of those ten years has produced superb records of these annual illustration showcases and each annual book surpasses the last. This one is no exception. Not only are we presenting the finest work of this year but we are also paying tribute to the illustrators of the past by presenting examples of the members of the Illustrators Hall of Fame.

But the Editor wanders. The point of my message is to say thank you to but a few of the men and women who have put this Annual together. To the juries, to Doug Cramer and his crew, to the staff at the Society, especially Arpi Ermoyan. To Terry Brown, Charles McVicker, and Jill Bossert for their fine articles, to Bob Hallock for his generous time and enormous talent, to Jerry McConnell for his patience, to Russ Neale and Jim Moore at Hastings House, and finally to the illustrators. Thank you all.

DESIGNER'S COMMENT by Robert Hallock

Subject: ILLUSTRATORS 22
Number of entries submitted to juries: 6199
Number accepted for the exhibition: 633

Result 1: The definite record of the best in contemporary illustration in all categories. *Result 2:* Setting new standards of excellence in the ever-evolving field of illustration with its challenges to create fresh interpretations of the world around us. *Result 3:* Providing mutual stimulus to artist and buyer to prove graphic creativity as a vital force in communication. *Result 4:* Expanding the visual world of constantly evaluating the best of what's been done to achieve ever new dimensions.

The endpapers are composed of a repeat pattern of the familiar S. I. insignia designed by Bradbury Thompson in 1960.

1968   Peter Helck

1969   Austin Briggs

1970   Rube Goldberg

HALL OF FAME—**HOWARD CHANDLER CHRISTY**

The Cafe Des Artistes just off Central Park West is like many elegant, intimate bistros in New York. But what distinguishes it from the others are the cascades of nymphets sporting in leafy glades all over the rooms. They are Howard Chandler Christy's girls, and they're a healthy lot. Christy loved peppy girls. He thought good skin, teeth and hair and lots of animation were the American ideal. He made the rest of the country think so too with his ubiquitous "Christy Girl."

From the turn of the century to 1921, his girls filled magazines, graced advertisements and posters and were the subject of a number of books. Thousands of young men enlisted in 1917 in response to a Christy poster that read, "Gee!! I wish I Were *a Man*." The model for that famous call to arms was Nancy Palmer, who became Christy's second wife in 1919. Norman Rockwell described her as, "a big, handsome, blonde woman who always reminded me of an 1890's burlesque queen." For her husband, she was the embodiment of the vision that had created the "Christy Girl."

Smiley, as Christy was called as a youngster, hadn't always drawn pretty girls. His first commission wasn't even of a woman. It was of a bull for the local butcher in Muskingum County, Ohio, when Christy was ten. All through his childhood, he sketched. He ended his formal education at 12 to draw and to help out on his father's farm. In 1889, when he was 16, he took $300 and made his way to New York to study at the Art Students League. His money ran out in short order so he

1971 Stevan Dohanos   1972 Ray Prohaska   1973 Jon Whitcomb

returned to the farm. Three years later, backed by a wealthy relative, he gave it another try, enrolling at the League and the National Academy. He showed such promise that William Merritt Chase took him on as a private student at his famous Tenth Street Studio.

Christy pursued fine art for five years until impecuniosity, coupled with a six dollar sale to *Life* magazine, convinced him to take up illustration. Chase, incensed, refused to speak to the struggling artist for three years. But Smiley's hardships came to an end in 1898. Reportage commissions to cover the Spanish-American war came from *Harper's*, *Scribner's* and *Leslie's Weekly*. Christy traveled with Teddy Roosevelt, sketching all the way; the result was a book called *Men of the Army and Navy*, published the following year. His record of most of the major action, including the Battle of Santiago, made him a celebrity.

Christy returned home to many assignments of a military nature. He complained, "Surely by now I have served my apprenticeship and have earned an opportunity of just one girl—*any* girl." But once again it was another soldier story. This time, however, he portrayed his first Christy girl in the curling smoke of the returning hero's pipe. Almost overnight he became one of the top dream-makers around.

One of his models, Maybelle Thompson, married him but the marriage was a tempestuous one amid much gossip. The marriage ended after ten years and Christy withdrew to Duncan Falls, Ohio with his daughter, Natalie, to recoup his

emotional health. He became a Christian Scientist and worked according to a strict regimen, (the imported models bivouacked in the many guestrooms) once completing 27 paintings in 28 days.

On his return to New York in 1915, he moved into the Hotel Des Artistes, one of the first of many artists to do so. In the thirties, the Cafe dedicated one of their rooms to him.

Christy was a boisterous, garrulous fellow. He and his buddy, James Montgomery Flagg, were the life of any party at the Players Club, the Aldine Club or the Lambs Club. The gossip columnists loved him and his opinions on beauty were cause for headlines. "'Not the 'V' But the Wearer Determines Modesty,' Says Illustrator Christy."

In 1921, the year of the first Miss America Beauty Contest in Atlantic City, Christy was the only judge. The following year he was joined by Coles Phillips, J. M. Flagg, Charles Chambers and Norman Rockwell. Rockwell said of Christy, "Publicity and he were right for each other. Like pearls and duchesses or cole slaw and church suppers."

It was also in 1921 that Christy was elected an honorary member of the U.S. Naval Academy. Christy was dedicated to a number of causes—the Police Athletic League, the Red Cross, the Salvation Army and the Children's Humane Society. And in 1921, at the peak of his career, he announced his retirement from illustration to become a portrait painter. That first year he completed 30 canvases which included Mrs. William Randolph Hearst and President Warren G. Harding. Over the years he painted and befriended a dazzling array of the rich and famous: Will Rogers, Herbert Hoover, Mary Baker Eddy, Norman Vincent Peale, the Prince of Wales, the Crown Prince of Italy, Amelia Earhart, Captain Eddie Rickenbacker and Mussolini.

For the sesquicentennial of the signing of the Constitution, (in 1937), Christy received a $30,000 commission to do a 20-by-30-foot canvas depicting the event. He spent two years researching and eight months in the Navy Yard sail loft painting the piece that now hangs above the east grand staircase in the Capitol. For the next decade, he did a number of large-scale historical murals in addition to his many portraits. With the onset of World War II, Christy's posters appeared once again but with less bounce and more sobriety than for the former war.

Howard Chandler Christy died in 1952 at 79, leaving an unfinished portrait of General Douglas MacArthur on his easel.

—*Jill Bossert*

1974   Charles Dana Gibson   1974   N. C. Wyeth   1974   Tom Lovell

HALL OF FAME—JAMES MONTGOMERY FLAGG

Monty was born with moxie. The date was June 18, 1877. Elisha and Anna's son grew up in Brooklyn and Manhattan and began working in the editorial offices of *St. Nicholas*, *Judge* and *Life*, ready markets for his humorous drawings. By 16, he was a regular contributor to the weeklies. The Art Students League offered more stimulating company than high school so he studied there for four years while he still sold his work to the weeklies.

In 1898, a year after he left the League, Flagg and Richard Kimbrough, a fellow League student, left for England, where they studied at Herkomer's Art School in Bushley and drew the Americans abroad. Flagg's *Yankee Girls* was published soon afterward by an English firm. This was the first step in the development of the "Flagg Girl." Kimbrough's untimely death ended their holiday and Flagg returned home.

The suddenness of Flagg's marriage to St. Louis socialite, Nellie McCormick, in 1899 has never been fully explained. Years his senior and raised in a loftier stratum, she appeared less wife than patron. For four years, Flagg and his wife traveled throughout the U.S. and Europe. With *Life* magazine's support, Flagg studied with Victor Marec in Paris. Flagg's studio portraits were exhibited in the salon shows. He and his wife returned to New York in 1904 to an apartment in the Hotel Des Artistes off Central Park West.

It was at this West 67th Street studio that illustrations rolled off his board at the rate of one per day. While he was adept at many media—including watercolor, oils and sculpture—he preferred the pen over all. *Harper's Weekly*, *The Saturday Evening Post*, *Liberty*, *McClure's*, *Century*, *Good Housekeeping* and *Scribner's* all helped to push Flagg's earnings to the top of his profession. He illustrated "Jeeves" by P. G. Wodehouse in *Collier's* for many years.

Flagg's illustrations were held in high esteem by such top writers of the day as Edna Ferber, W. S. Hart, Julian Street, Booth Tarkington, Sinclair Lewis and George Barr McCutcheon. Flagg's favorite writer, though, was himself. His writings exhibited a witty sense of the ridiculous as he poked fun at nearly every established convention; Nervy Nat (a *Judge* series), satirical short stories, screenplays, the Dutch Treat Club's annual presentation and the Society of Illustrators' smokers and girlie shows were a few of Flagg's literary forums. During one period, he found time to write 24 short screenplays, a weekly syndicated column and a Broadway play.

When America entered into WW I, illustrators rallied

1975   Maxfield Parrish

1975   Howard Pyle

1975   Bernard Fuchs

around the banner of Charles Dana Gibson's Division of Pictorial Publicity. Flagg, who had already created the "I Want You" image for *Leslie's Weekly*, proceeded to design 46 posters for the war effort. During WW II, Flagg's Uncle Sam reemerged and could be found in front of every post office and recruiting station across the country.

The period between these wars found James Montgomery Flagg at a social pinnacle. He had moved his studio to 57th Street and summered in Maine. *Harper's* magazine wrote of him: "although his industry appears appalling, he does not lack an abundance of leisure." He took this leisure with the Barrymores, the Roosevelts, the fellows of his many clubs and a long list of Hollywood starlets. They were honored to be the brunt of a Flagg comment or the subject of a humorous or serious portrait. Rosalind Russell said of hers, "You certainly can paint, you old bastard!"

The period between the wars also found Flagg's personal life in turmoil. Nellie died in 1923 and he married Dorothy Wadman the following year. The second Mrs. Flagg, who was the mother of his only child, Faith, suffered a nervous collapse and was hospitalized for the rest of her life. He never remarried.

J. M. Flagg was 48 years old at the time of his daughter's birth. His lifestyle was not perfectly suited to raise a child but as a single parent he did his best. Flagg adored Faith and she was a frequent model for him as she grew through the years. His portraits of her record a softer side of Flagg's personality.

Flagg was a character "both loved and hated with equal fierceness." He detested sham and pretense. His retorts caught the unwary off-guard and hardened his friends. In Flagg's later years, when his failing eyesight forced him to abandon his art, he often took out his frustrations on his friends and himself. "I've always been more interested in battling life today, than in trying to build a dead tomorrow." After two heart attacks, near blindness, Monty died in 1960 at age 82. Dean Cornwell, Arthur William Brown, Jack Dempsey and Flagg's close friend, Everett Raymond Kinstler were among those at the funeral. Kinstler said of Monty: "Everthing he did was as uniquely Flagg as his manner of speaking or his eyebrows. He loved beauty and he loved laughter." He told me, "If the cerulean brass hats ever send me to heaven, and I find no laughter, I will get to Hell out of there." It is unlikely that we will see another James Montgomery Flagg.

—*Terry Brown*

1976   Winslow Homer

1976   Harvey Dunn

1976   John Falter

HALL OF FAME—**SAUL TEPPER**

1977   Wallace Morgan

1977   J. C. Leyendecker

1977   Robert Peak

SANDOR ACS

A very special child was born to eastern European immigrants Max and Sarah Tepper on Christmas Day, 1899, on the lower east side of Manhattan. New York's melting pot is well known for the talents that emerged from those streets of pushcarts and immigrants. Hard work was the key to success there, and Saul Tepper was no exception. By 19, he was working full time in his own lettering studio while studying art at night and on weekends. He found William DeLeftwich Dodge's composition classes at Cooper Union and George Bridgeman's "ideas in drawing" at the Art Students League, were important influences. But his most important influence came later, under Harvey Dunn at the Grand Central Art School and at Dunn's Tenafly, New Jersey, studio.

After graduating from Cooper Union, Saul acquired a job in a studio as a lettering man. There, he had his first chance to do some figure work in oil. In 1920, he married Beatrice Lindenburg. They had two children, Albert and Joan. In 1925, at the Van Dyke Studios he branched out as an illustrator. For the next few years, his work developed under the guidance of Harvey Dunn. Saul's first sample from his new studio was purchased by *Liberty* magazine, who created a story around it. *Collier's* followed shortly thereafter, as did the Curtis Publishing group (*Ladies Home Journal*, *Saturday Evening Post* and *Country Gentleman*) then came *Woman's Home Companion*, *The American*, *Cosmopolitan* and *Good Housekeeping*. By the mid 1930's, Saul's style had become recognizable and commanded top dollar. His advertising campaigns for Chesterfield cigarettes and General Electric and his WW II posters, commissioned by the United States government and by Stetson Hats, are most notable.

Saul moved his work to the Lincoln Square Studios and then, for thirteen of his most productive years, to the Hotel Des Artistes.

A multifaceted talent, Saul branched out into other fields. Aside from his masterful use of the brush, Saul had a strong love of music which has led to many published songs and resulted in a membership in ASCAP in 1941. He created many of the songs for the popular "Illustrators Shows," produced by the Society of Illustrators. The Illustrators Barbershop Quartet, with Saul as baritone, was a highlight of those productions. Over the years, Saul's music has been recorded by Nat King Cole, Ella Fitzgerald, Glenn Miller, Harry James and many others.

As a lecturer, Saul has spoken often to groups of students and professionals at Cooper Union, Pratt Institute, the Society of Illustrators and Art Directors Clubs.

Because Saul knows the importance of the patient help one artist will lend another, he has given of his time to many. Al Dorne apprenticed to Saul at his first lettering studio and later Harry Beckoff and others. We will never know how many would have put down the pen for a shovel without Saul's help. He tells about one young man, Arthur DeKuh, an ex-boxer and bathhouse bouncer, who, through hard work and Saul's critiques, established a career in art.

Saul, having grown up during the Golden Age of American Illustration, was influenced by it. The period between World War I and II was Saul's "Golden Age," an era of romance and adventure in which he, Cornwell and Rockwell played an important part. Reproduced in the major magazines for four decades, Saul's work became a source of inspiration for many artists of that period.

In the 1950's, still an active artist for the new adventure magazines (*True*, *Argosy* and *Real*), Saul reached a point of dissatisfaction. He became TV art director for J. Walter Thompson and BBD&O, creating images for TV commercials. He also continued with his music, composing the Red Cross theme song for 1960-1961. Now Saul is on another venture—restoring his paintings and inventing tools for the process. No one will ever think of Saul as retired.

The world of illustration is indeed fortunate that Saul Tepper embraced this artform with his sensitivity, intelligence and energy.

— *Terry Brown*

1978 Norman Price

1978 Frederic Remington

1978 Coby Whitmore

ROSEMARY HOWARD

HAMILTON KING AWARD—**WILSON McLEAN**

At first glance Wilson McLean is boyish, winsome. His eyes, however, reveal the seriousness of his intent. He is a very intense man. One suspects that he was a very intense boy in Scotland where he was born. While his parents worked in a local laundry he would draw on the end pages of his mother's cook books, the only white paper around. Pavement chalk drawing was a popular art on the streets of Glasgow and Wilson, age five, was on his knees doing portraits of Hitler, Tojo, FDR and Churchill. He *always* wanted to be an artist. Though she couldn't envision how someone could make a living, his mother didn't quash his enthusiasm. When he was ten, a year after the family moved outside London, she sent him to a local teacher for lessons. In a year the McLeans moved again and the lessons stopped, but Wilson didn't. Instead of cricket and soccer, he copied the comics, in particular the well-known D. C. Eyles.

He left school at 15 and went to work as an assistant to a sign painter. It was this training that left him with the ability to render tight, straight lines—without masking tape—a recognizable feature of his work today. He worked in various silkscreen shops and small commercial art studios until he was 18. With romantic visions of foreign climes he joined the R.A.F. and spent two hideous years in the Middle East where the only artwork he did was to paint trucks and decorate the bar on base.

Upon his return to London and without any previous experience, he took a job doing layout for a woman's magazine. In his words, "Sheer desperation is the key to so much of what we do." What he began by faking, he soon learned. As he did he

1979   Edwin A. Abbey

1979   Lorraine Fox

1979   Ben Stahl

was also exposed to the top American illustrators. They knocked him out—men like Coby Whitmore, Joe Bowler, Bob Peak and especially Tom Allen, Bob Weaver and, most of all, Bernie Fuchs. Wilson went free-lance when he was 24. After two hard years he became well enough established for his rep to say he was cutting his own throat by packing up and going to America. He didn't listen and came to New York intending to stay five years. He discovered he could do things here that he couldn't do in England and Europe. It's been 14 years, and though he still considers that he's here on a visit, he's become a permanent fixture in American illustration.

Wilson has been handed every conceivable assignment, from fashion for *Playboy*, (in which it was necessary to insert a small portion of a woman's torso on each completed canvas in compliance with their naked lady policy), to a graphic rendition of anxiety, a difficult task he made even more challenging by not using any figures. One of the most demanding jobs he did was an animated commercial for Eastern Airlines. For three solid months he was up to his eyebrows in flamingos and palm trees; he was rewarded with a "Clio."

With his extraordinary skills and imagination Wilson McLean is a risk taker. Perhaps because of his lack of formal training he isn't aware that there are things one isn't supposed to do. When he gets an assignment his first thought is, "How far can I take this?" Within the confines of the client's needs just how far can he stretch? A *Sports Illustrated* story about cock fighting becomes a surreal experience of sweat and blood-letting set in an elegant, formal graphic. An exotic drink for a bartenders' association is illustrated by a perfect wave coming from a perfect shell witnessed by the perfect bon vivant, and not a cocktail glass in sight. Wilson works long, intense hours in his fabulous loft which he shares with his wife, Rosemary Howard. He's got his art studio, she's got her photography studio and his two teen-agers, Karin and Sean, share both when they're home.

The Society would like to thank Dick Gangel of *Sports Illustrated* for giving Wilson the story, "We know of Knute, yet know him not," about football in the days of Knute Rockne. It was from this series that the Hamilton King Award emerged. And we'd like to watch Wilson McLean continue to take risks, be it in Zurich doing his own prints, or in a thousand perfect Perrier bubbles.

—*Jill Bossert*

THE SOCIETY OF ILLUSTRATORS MUSEUM OF AMERICAN ILLUSTRATION

On February 2, 1981 at 6:30 P.M. the tape was cut, officially opening the lower gallery at the Society of Illustrators. The first exhibit utilizing both galleries was Illustrators 23 and the opening signified that the new Society of Illustrators Museum of American Illustration now had space, tangible room in which to exist.

The new gallery is the finest development at the Society since the Annual Exhibit was begun 23 years ago. Illustrations are now collectibles and hung in bona fide galleries. It is time for illustration to be enshrined and the entire museum is dedicated to that end.

Collecting illustrations is not new to the Society. All during its history, the Society has collected the work of its members— first in the Presidents' collection and later, in a more general way, from members who were willing to donate. For years some of the collection hung in the dining and founders' rooms, while the rest gathered dust in the basement. John Moodie was curator for this collection. He and Terry Brown gave loving and respectful care to the restoration and framing of the precious collection.

Lila Acheson Wallace provided funds to create a suitable storage room above what once was a stage at the rear of the first floor gallery. There was now the nucleus of a fine assemblage of American illustration and a good place to store it.

Events in other areas had led to the inevitable stewardship by the Society as caretaker of illustration's history. In 1966 Estelle and Bette Mandel had officially established the Museum of Illustrative Art and raised funds to create such an institution. With the death of Estelle Mandel, the concept was held for a time to grow.

In the spring of 1976, the first exhibit selected from the permanent collection left our building to be shown in the Master Eagle Gallery in celebration of the Society's 75th Anniversary. In a fresh space, the collection's beauty and value could be seen anew.

In the fall of 1976, the momentous *200 Years of American Illustration* exhibit opened at the New York Historical Society. Many pieces from the permanent collection were exhibited and took their places on authorized museum walls gracefully and honorably.

The Society formed a committee headed by John Witt to develop the museum concept and bring it to fruition. And, by God, the committee did. A direction had been decided. An illustrated brochure for the new museum was created and the fund raising began. Who best to ask first for contributions but the members of the Society, and they responded gloriously, 250 strong.

And then the windfall. J. Walter Thompson, the largest ad agency in the world, showed its faith in and esteem for illustration by contributing a large sum of money, making the cutting of the ribbon a possibility. John Moodie was instrumental in bringing this about. An architect was commissioned, and designs for the new gallery were approved, even before the funds were raised. The Society was ready. Gerald McConnell worked swiftly and imaginatively as coordinator of the project. The results speak for themselves. The dank basement has been transformed.

Brilliant ideas always seem inevitable, but they are not. Most often they are the culmination of many small and large events and the sweat of many fine people. This was the case as the Society grandly opened its new museum space. It's still just a beginning, but the potential is great. It is an important beginning and will be so recorded.

— *Charles McVicker*

1
Advertising
Artist: **Fred Otnes**
Art Director: Todd Hoon
Agency: Zimmer, McClaskey, Lewis, Inc.
Client: Brown & Williamson Tobacco Co.

2
Editorial
Artist: **James Endicott**
Art Director: Joe Brooks
Publication: Penthouse Magazine

3
Editorial
Artist: **Al Hirschfeld**
Art Director: Nicki Kalish
Publication: New York Times

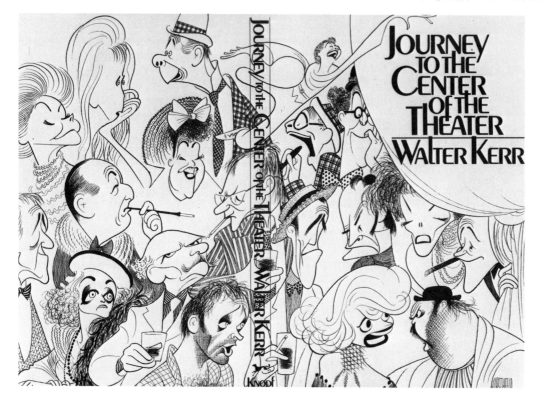

4
Book
Artist: **Al Hirschfeld**
Art Director: Lidia Ferrara
Title: Journey to the Center of the Theater
Publisher: Alfred A. Knopf, Inc.

5
Editorial
Artist: **Chuck Slack**
Art Director: Carol Rasmussen
Publication: Chicago Tribune

6
Editorial
Artist: **Chuck Slack**
Art Director: Dan Jursa
Publication: Chicago Tribune Magazine

7
Book
Artist: **Alan Reingold**
Art Director: Jack Tauss
Publisher: The Franklin Library

8
Editorial
Artist: **Don Ivan Punchatz**
Art Director: Joe Brooks
Publication: Penthouse Magazine

9
Editorial
Artist: **Marshall Arisman**
Art Directors: Arthur Paul/Len Willis
Publication: Playboy Magazine

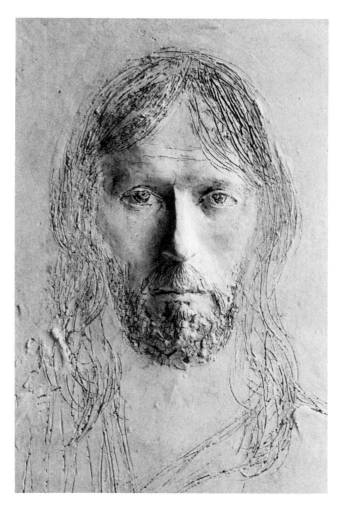

10
Advertising
Artist: **Miriam Brofsky**
Art Director: Murlin Marsh
Client: NBC

11
Institutional
Artist: **Richard Newton**
Art Director: Richard Newton

12
Editorial
Artist: **Birney Lettick**
Art Directors: Walter Bernard/Rudy Hoglund
Publication: Time Magazine

13
Editorial
Artist: **Mike Presley**
Art Director: Joe Brooks
Publication: Penthouse Magazine

14
Institutional
Artist: **Gary Kelley**
Art Director: Gary Kelley
Client: Hellman Design Associates

15
Editorial
Artist: **Ed Soyka**
Art Director: Robert Priest
Publication: Weekend Magazine

16
Editorial
Artist: **Marvin Mattelson**
Art Director: Carveth Kramer
Publication: Psychology Today

17
Book
Artist: **Lou Glanzman**
Art Director: Len Leone
Title: Young Adolph
Publisher: Bantam Books, Inc.

18
Editorial
Artist: **Mark Skolsky**
Art Director: Mark Skolsky

19
Editorial
Artist: **Burt Silverman**
Art Directors: Walter Bernard/Rudy Hoglund
Publication: Time Magazine

20
Advertising
Artist: **Birney Lettick**
Art Directors: Bill Gold/Tal Stubis
Agency: Bill Gold Advertising
Client: Malpaso Co./Paramount Pictures

21
Editorial
Artist: **Daniel Maffia**
Art Directors: Mary Shanahan/Greg Scott
Publication: Rolling Stone

22
Advertising
Artist: **Scott Reynolds**
Art Director: Jack Tauss
Client: The Franklin Library

23
Editorial
Artist: **Michael Leonard**
Art Directors: Walter Bernard/Rudy Hoglund
Publication: Time Magazine

24
Editorial
Artist: **Nancy Ohanian**
Art Director: Tim Rutten
Publication: Los Angeles Times

25
Editorial
Artist: **Gerry Gersten**
Art Director: Irene Ramp
Publication: Time Magazine

26
Institutional
Artist: **Gerry Gersten**
Art Director: Sam Antupit
Client: Quality Paperback Book Club

27
Editorial
Artist: **Richard Hess**
Art Director: Ed Schneider
Client: Washington Post Magazine

28
Book
Artist: **Hodges Soileau**
Art Director: Rich Carter
Agency: MBI (Books Division)
Publisher: Eastern Press

29
Editorial
Artist: **Richard Krepel**
Art Director: Alice Degenhardt
Publication: Creative Living Magazine

30
Editorial
Artist: **Jim Sharpe**
Art Director: Dave Moore
Agency: International Communication Agency
Client: Soviet Union Distribution

31
Institutional
Artist: **Michael Dudash**
Art Director: Michael Dudash

32
Book
Artist: **Bob Crofut**
Art Director: Richard Carter
Title: The Brothers Karamazov
Publisher: The Easton Press, M.B.I.

33
Book
Artist: **Edward W. Acuña**
Art Director: Richard Carter
Publisher: Heritage Books

34
Institutional
Artist: **William Ersland**
Art Director: William Ersland
Client: Hellman Design Assocs.

35
Editorial
Artist: **Daniel Schwartz**
Art Director: Ron Campbell
Publication: Fortune Magazine
Gold Medal

36
Editorial
Artist: **Frank Morris**
Art Director: Jean Claude Suarès
Publication: New York Magazine

37
Editorial
Artist: **Richard Hess**
Art Directors: Walter Bernard/Rudy Hoglund
Publication: Time Magazine

38
Editorial
Artist: **Burt Silverman**
Art Directors: Walter Bernard/Rudy Hoglund
Publication: Time Magazine

39
Editorial
Artist: **Jim Campbell**
Art Directors: Don Duffy/Don Hedin
Publication: Reader's Digest

40
Editorial
Artist: **Bernie Fuchs**
Art Director: Jerry Alten
Publication: TV Guide

41
Book
Artist: **Ben F. Stahl**
Art Director: Jack Tauss
Publisher: Franklin Library

42
Advertising
Artist: **Chuck Wilkinson**
Art Director: Doug Fisher
Agency: Lord, Sullivan & Yoder
Client: Nevamar Corporation

43
Institutional
Artist: **Gregory Manchess**
Art Director: Gary Kelley
Agency: Hellman Design Assoc.
Client: Hellman Design Assoc.

44
Book
Artist: **Bob Lapsley**
Art Director: Jim Plumeri
Title: The Adventures of Tom Sawyer and
        The Adventures Of Huckleberry Finn
Publisher: New American Library

45
Book
Artist: **Richard Sparks**
Art Director: Rich Carter
Title: War and Peace
Publisher: Easton Press
Client: MBI, Inc.

46
Advertising
Artist: **Chet Jezierski**
Art Director: Stan Sweeney
Agency: W. B. Doner & Co.
Client: National Guard

47
Institutional
Artist: **Tom Bookwalter**
Art Director: Tom Bookwalter
Client: Hellman Design

48
Editorial
Artist: **Gary Kelley**
Art Director: Greg Schultz
Publication: Webb Publishing—
    Passages Magazine

49
Editorial
Artist: **Julian Allen**
Art Director: Bea Feitler
Publication: Rolling Stone

50
Institutional
Artist: **Barron Storey**
Art Director: Wayne Roth
Agency: Corpcom Services, Inc.
Client: Coca Cola

51
Institutional
Artist: **Fred Otnes**
Art Director: Joseph Smith
Agency: Garrison Jasper & Rose Co.
Client: Kawneer

52
Advertising
Artist: **Fred Otnes**
Art Director: Todd Hoon
Agency: Zimmer, McClaskey & Lewis Inc.
Client: Brown & Williamson Tobacco Co.

53
Editorial
Artist: **Larry Winborg**
Art Director: Lorraine Brod
Publication: Hospital Publications

54
Editorial
Artist: **Jim Butcher**
Art Director: Vince Maiello
Publisher: Playboy Books

55
Advertising
Artist: **Judith Jampel**
Art Director: Steven Johnson
Agency: Wray-Ward Advertising
Client: Ciba Geigy Dye-Stuffs Div.

56
Advertising
Artist: **Richard Waldrep**
Art Director: Tom Burden
Agency: Mathis, Burden & Charles
Client: Baltimore Convention Center

57
Book
Artist: **Hodges Soileau**
Art Director: Rich Carter
Agency: MBI (Books Division)
Publisher: Eastern Press

58
Advertising
Artist: **Barron Storey**
Art Director: Alan Davis
Client: London Records

59
Book
Artist: **John Thompson**
Art Director: Len Leone
Title: A Rockwell Portrait
Publisher: Bantam Books, Inc.

60
TV
Artist: **Tim Boxell**
Art Director: Damon Rarey
Client: "Over Easy" KQED, Inc.

61
Advertising
Artist: **Jack Unruh**
Art Director: Jack Unruh

62
Advertising
Artist: **Jack Unruh**
Art Director: Jack Unruh

63
Advertising
Artist: **Jerry Dadds**
Art Director: Jerry Dadds
Client: Eucalyptus Tree Studio

64
Book
Artist: **Joan Hall**
Art Director: Barbara Bertoli
Title: Louisa May/A Modern Biography
Publisher: Avon Books

65
Advertising
Artist: **Edward J. Abrams**
Art Director: Marvin Schwartz
Client: Angel Records

66
Advertising
Artist: **Mel Odom**
Art Director: Henrietta Condak
Client: CBS Records

The Desperate Husband
An opera by
Domenico Cimarosa
The American Premiere at
Spoleto Festival 1979
Charleston, S.C.
Made possible in part by
a grant from Mobil

67
Advertising
Artist: **Ivan Chermayeff**
Agency: Chermayeff & Geismar Assoc.
Client: Mobil Oil Corporation

Principal Subsidiaries or Divisions / Products & Systems

COMPONENTS

Power Transmission Components

Principal Subsidiaries or Divisions	Products & Systems
Bolenz & Schaefer GmbH & Co. KG Eckelshausen, West Germany	Hydraulic piston accumulators, filament winding machines and tube elbow bending presses.
Dortmund, West Germany	Couplings, clutches, torque limiters and other mechanical power transmission components
Koshin-Racine, Ltd. Tokyo, Japan	Hydraulic pumps, valves and power units.
Racine Hidraulica S.A. Porto Alegre, Brazil	Hydraulic pumps, cylinders, valves and power units.
Racine Rex Div. of Rexnord GmbH Liederbach, West Germany	Sales engineering office, manufacturing of power units, component distribution.
Racine Rex. S.A. Houilles, France	Sales engineering office, manufacturing of power units, component distribution.
Rexnord B.V. Athlone, Republic of Ireland	Agricultural knives and blades
Rexnord Correntes Ltda. San Leopolodo, Brazil	Roller, agricultural, conveyor, TableTop, leaf and engineered steel chains.
Rexnord Australia Pty. Ltd. Sydney, Australia	Fabricated steel conveyor chain
Rexnord Kette GmbH & Co. KG Betzdorf, West Germany Hagen (Filey), West Germany Paris, France	Roller, agricultural, conveyor, TableTop, plastic, leaf and engineered steel chains.

Specialty Fasteners

Camloc Fastener GmbH Kelkhein/Taunus, West Germany	Quick opening specialty fasteners.
Camloc Ind. Fixings (U.K.) Ltd. Leicester, England	Quick opening specialty fasteners.
Camloc. France S.a.r.L. Paris, France	Quick opening specialty fasteners.

MACHINERY

Process Machinery

Ateliers Bergeaud-Macon, S.A. Macon, France	Jaw, gyratory and cone crushers, grizzlies, screens, vibrating feeders, bucket elevators, belt conveyors and engineering services.
Nordberg Industrial Ltda. Belo Horizonte, Brazil	Gyratory and cone crushers and screens.
Nordberg Mfg. Co. S.A. Pty. Ltd. Vereeninging, South Africa Alrode, South Africa Welkom, South Africa	Jaw, gyratory and cone crushers and screens.
Process Machinery Division Rexnord (Branch) London, England	Crushers and screens for processing metallic and nonmetallic ore, minerals, rock, sand and gravel. Specialty Chemicals including epoxy resins for backing wear materials.

Construction Machinery

Arbau International S.A. Paris, France	Concrete plant equipment.
Rex Arbau Div. of Rexnord GmbH Heidelberg, West Germany	Concrete plant equipment.

Rexnord

Rexnord Inc., P.O. Box 2022, Milwaukee, WI 53201
Bulletin 80139   Printed in U.S.A.

Capabilities to meet the needs of industry world-wide

69
Institutional
Artist: **Mark English**
Art Director: Mike Smollin
Client: Illustrators Workshop
Gold Medal

70
Advertising
Artist: **Robert Tanenbaum**
Art Director: Mike Salisbury
Agency: Wells Rich & Green
Client: Columbia Pictures

71
Advertising
Artist: **Ed Sorel**
Art Director: Susan Lyster
Agency: McCaffrey & McCall
Client: Exxon Corp.

72
Editorial
Artist: **Richard Amsel**
Art Director: Jerry Alten
Publication: TV Guide

73
Editorial
Artist: **Richard Amsel**
Art Director: Jerry Alten
Publication: TV Guide

74
Editorial
Artist: **Richard Amsel**
Art Director: Jerry Alten
Publication: TV Guide

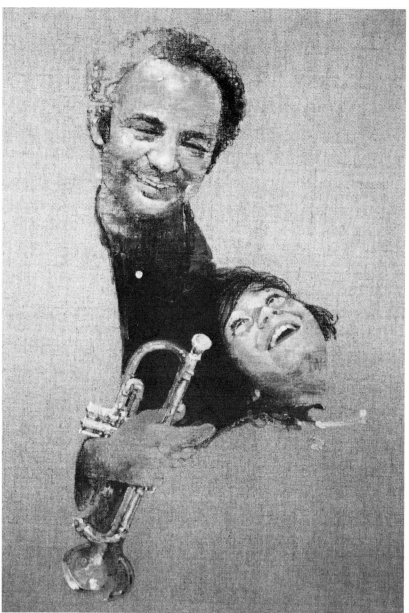

75
Advertising
Artist: **Robert Heindel**
Art Director: Burt Kleeger
Agency: J. Caroff Assocs.
Client: United Artists

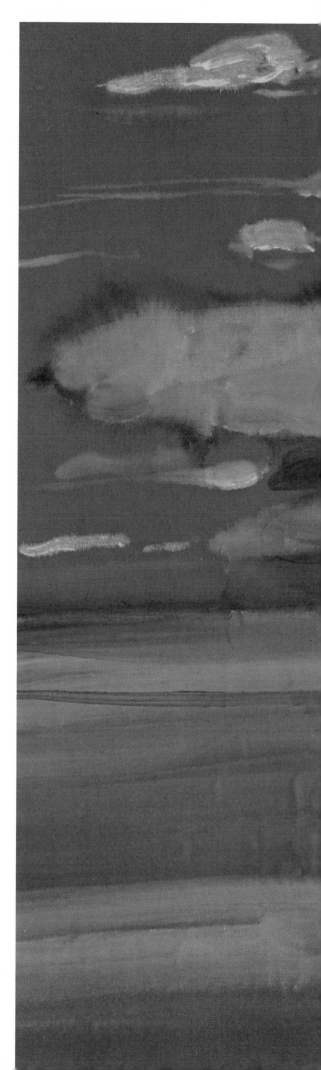

76
Advertising
Artist: **Robert Andrew Parker**
Art Director: John Berg
Client: CBS Records

Thelonious
Monk

Always
Know

77
Institutional
Artist: **Malcolm T. Liepke**
Art Director: Malcolm T. Liepke

78
Advertising
Artist: **Mel Odom**
Art Director: Henrietta Condak
Client: CBS Records

79
Advertising
Artist: **John Alcorn**
Art Directors: Paula Scher/Andrea Klein
Client: CBS Records

81
Advertising
Artist: **Daniel Schwartz**
Art Director: Donald S. Komai
Client: Time-Life Books

80
Advertising
Artist: **John Collier**
Art Directors: Johnny Lee/Ron Coro
Client: Elektra/Asylum Records
Gold Medal

82
Advertising
Artist: **Mark Hess**
Art Director: Gene Greif
Client: CBS Records

83
Advertising
Artist: **Mark Hess**
Art Director: Lynn Dreese Breslin
Client: Atlantic Records

84
Advertising
Artist: **Bob Weaver**
Art Director: Henrietta Condak
Client: CBS Records

85
Advertising
Artist: **Karen Faryniak**
Art Director: Karen Faryniak

86
Advertising
Artist: **Mark English**
Art Director: Donald S. Komai
Publisher: Time-Life Books

87
Advertising
Artist: **Bart Forbes**
Art Directors: Tom Clemente, John Sullivan
Agency: Newspaper Advertising Bureau
Client: Member Newspapers

88
Editorial
Artist: **Frank Morris**
Art Director: Fred Woodward
Publication: Memphis Magazine

89
Institutional
Artist: **Ivan Powell**
Art Director: Ivan Powell
Client: Jacqueline Dedell

90
Advertising
Artist: **David Wilcox**
Art Director: Lynn Dreese Breslin
Client: Atlantic Records
Gold Medal

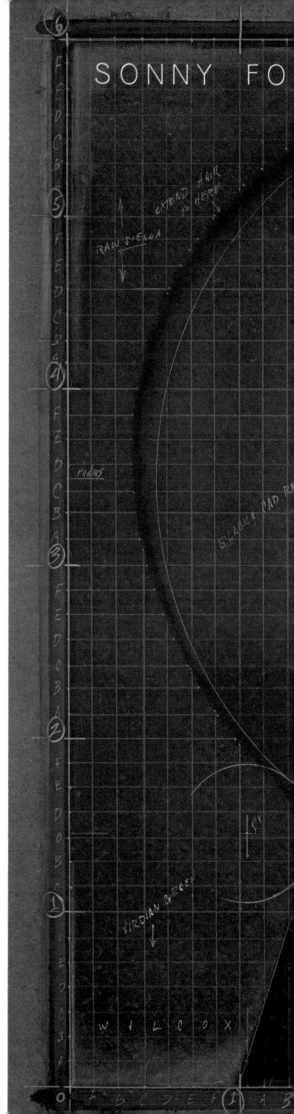

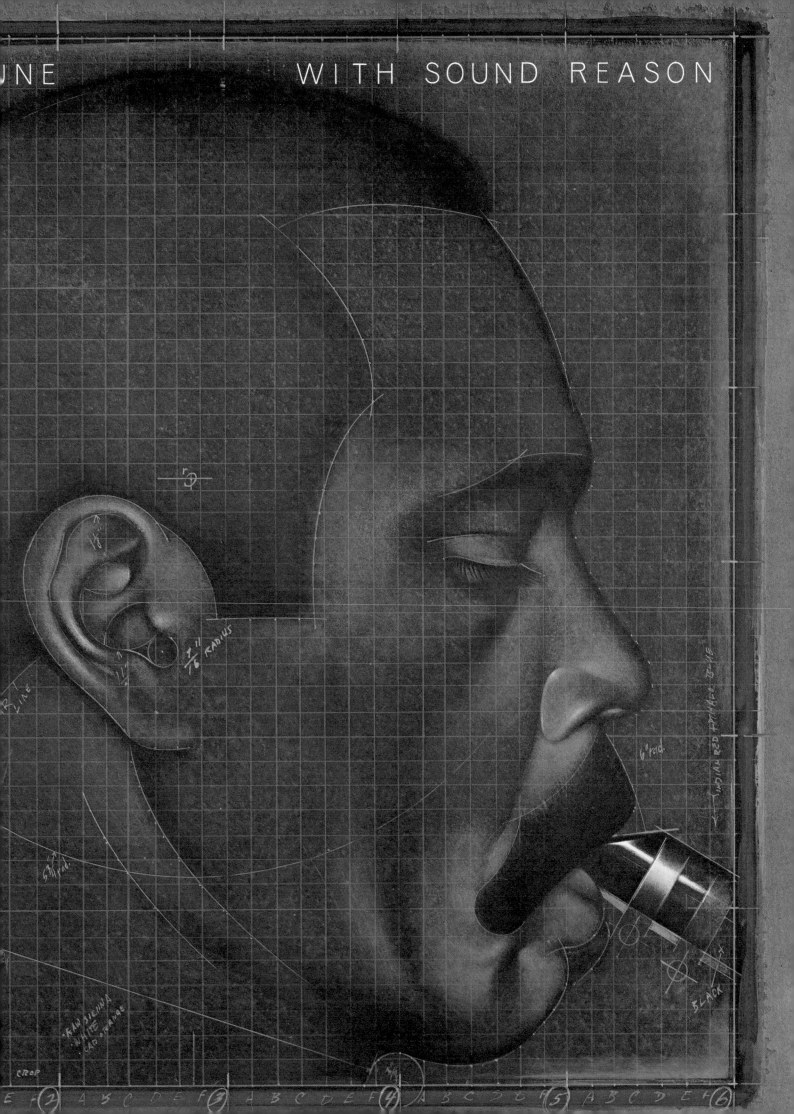

91
Editorial
Artist: **Edward J. Abrams**
Art Director: Edward J. Abrams

92
Editorial
Artist: **Susan Stillman**
Art Director: Jean Claude Suarès
Publication: New York Magazine

94
Advertising
Artist: **Mark Bellerose**
Art Director: Dave Lizotte
Agency: Gunn Associates
Client: Zildjian Co.

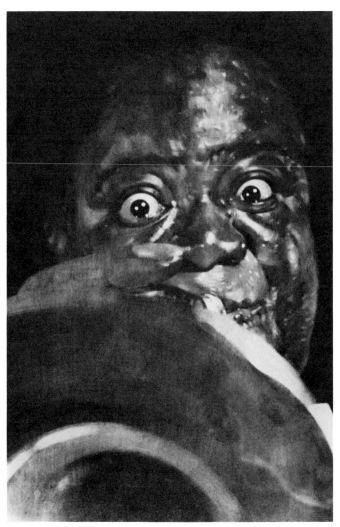

93
Book
Artist: **Bill Dula**
Art Director: Bill Dula
Title: "Louis"
Publisher: Pinnacle Books

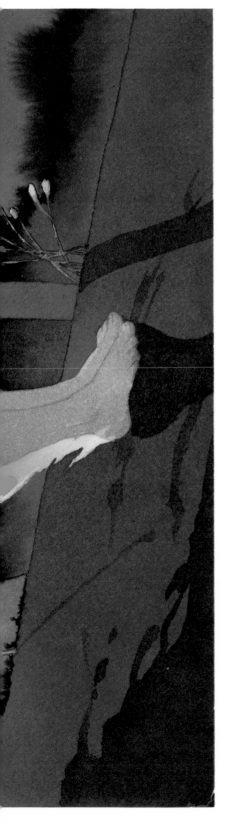

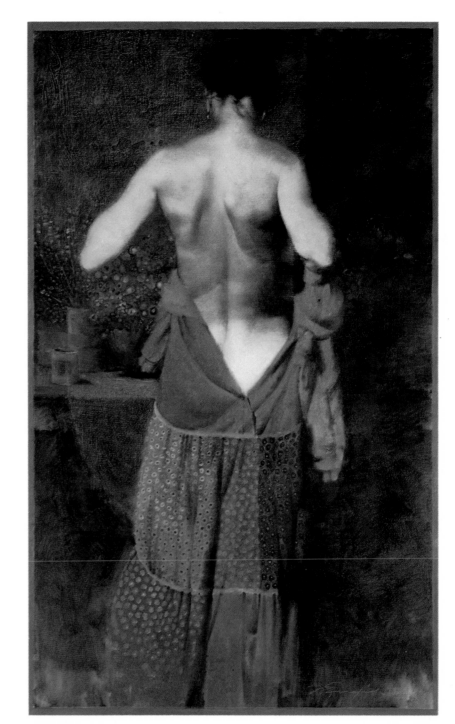

96
Advertising
Artist: **Mark English**
Art Director: Tim Trabon
Agency: Trabon Prints
Client: O'Grady Gallery
Gold Medal

95
Advertising
Artist: **Milton Glaser**
Art Director: Milton Glaser
Agency: Milton Glaser, Inc.
Client: The Tomato Music Co.

98
Book
Artist: **Sandy Kossin**
Art Director: Leonard Leone
Title: Is There Sex After Death
Publisher: Bantam Books, Inc

97
Advertising
Artist: **Al Hirschfeld**
Art Director: Henrietta Condak
Client: CBS Records

99
Advertising
Artist: **Cliff Condak**
Art Director: Henrietta Condak
Client: CBS Records

100
Advertising
Artist: **Cliff Condak**
Art Director: Henrietta Condak
Client: CBS Records

101
Institutional
Artist: **Malcolm T. Liepke**
Art Director: Malcolm T. Liepke

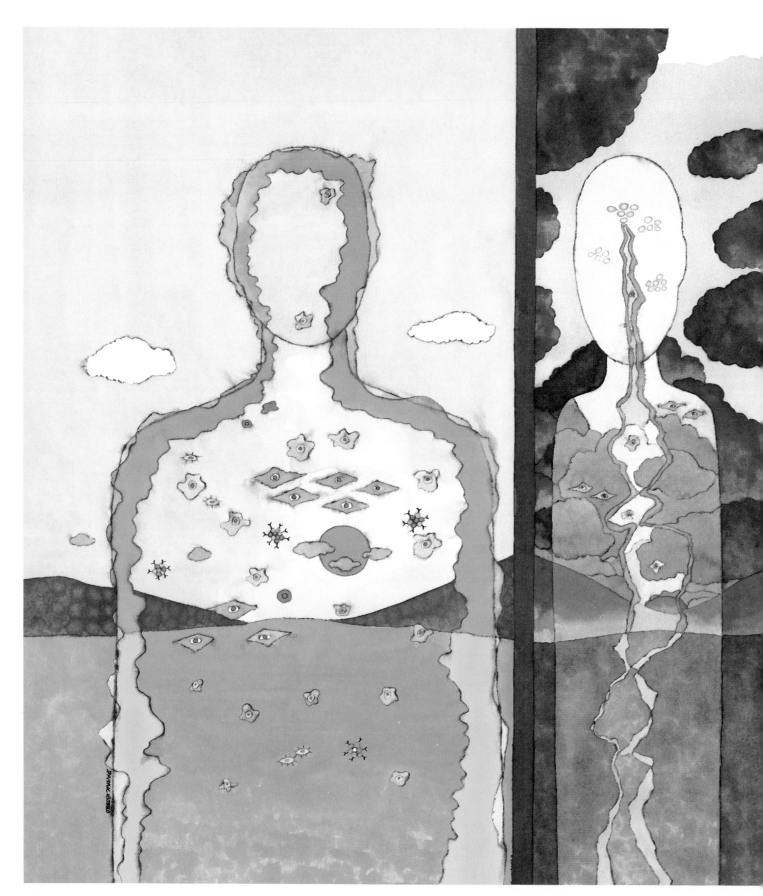

102
Editorial
Artist: **Frank Bozzo**
Art Directors: John deCesare/Tina Adamek
Agency: deCesare Design
Publisher: McGraw-Hill Inc.

103
Editorial
Artist: **Bob Ziering**
Art Director: Patrick Flynn
Publication: The Runner Magazine

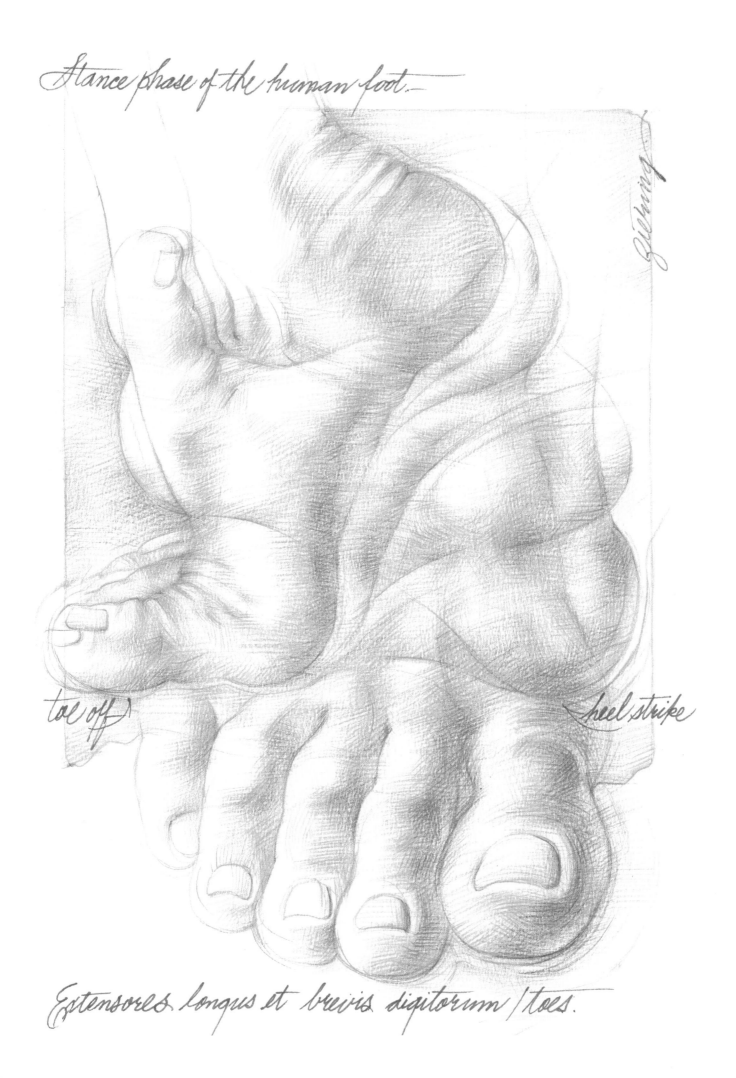

Stance phase of the human foot.

Giebling

toe off

heel strike

Extensores longus et brevis digitorum / toes.

104
Advertising
Artist: **Peter Cross**
Art Director: Alan Davis
Client: London Records

105
Editorial
Artist: **Malcolm T. Liepke**
Art Director: Malcolm T. Liepke

106
Advertising
Artist: **John Collier**
Art Directors: Henrietta Condak/Mark Handel
Client: CBS Records

107
Institutional
Artist: **Paul Orlando**
Art Director: Paul Orlando
Client: Maritz Motivation

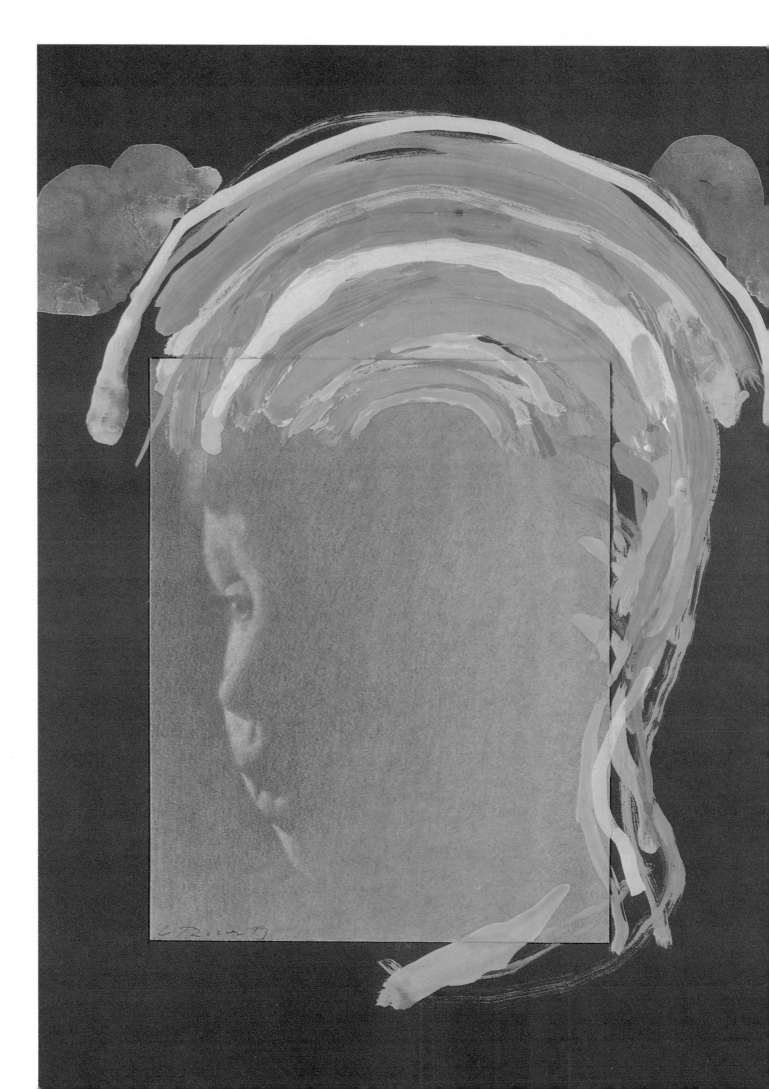

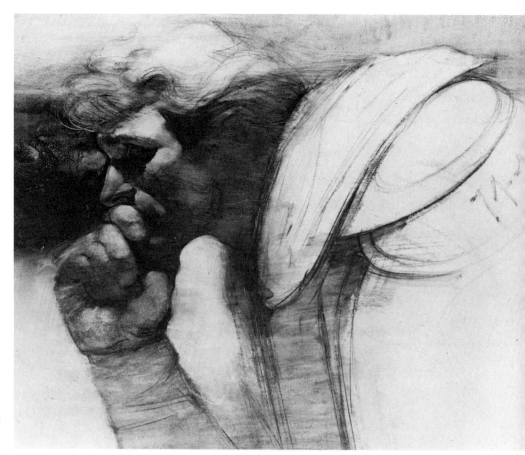

109
Book
Artist: **Richard MacDonald**
Art Director: Barbara Bertoli
Title: Joiner
Publisher: Avon Books

108
Advertising
Artist: **Liam Roberts**
Art Director: John Barban
Agency: John Barban Productions
Client: Learning Corp. of America

110
Editorial
Artist: **Jeffrey Schrier**
Art Director: Carveth Hilton Kramer
Publication: Psychology Today

111
Institutional
Artist: **William Ersland**
Art Director: William Ersland
Client: Hellman Design

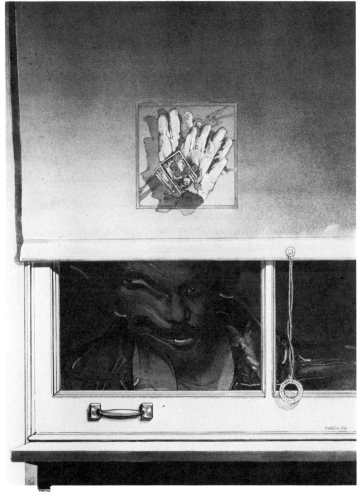

112
Editorial
Artist: **Frank Morris**
Art Director: Fred Woodward
Publication: Memphis Magazine

113
Institutional
Artists: **Seymour Chwast** and **Richard Mantel**
Art Director: Seymour Chwast
Agency: Push Pin Graphic
Client: Push Pin Graphic

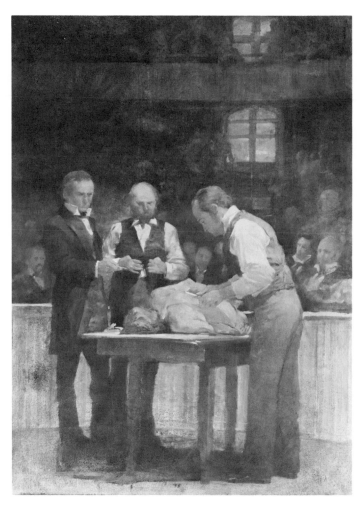

114
Book
Artist: **Stan Hunter**
Art Director: Tom VonDerLinn
Title: The Cry & the Covenant
Publisher: Reader's Digest

115
Book
Artist: **Stan Hunter**
Art Director: Tom VonDerLinn
Title: The Cry & the Covenant
Publisher: Reader's Digest

116
Institutional
Artist: **Susan M. Blubaugh**
Art Director: Susan M. Blubaugh

117
Advertising
Artist: **Larry Kresek**
Art Director: Jay Forman
Agency: Sudler & Hennessey, Inc.
Client: Ayerst Laboratories

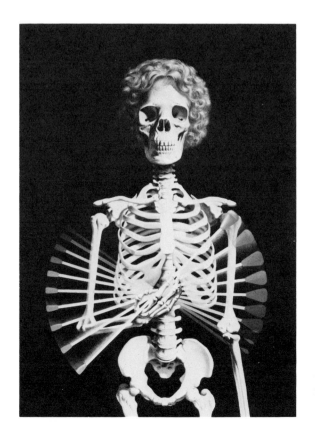

118
Book
Artist: **Howard Koslow**
Art Director: Milton Charles
Title: The Majorettes
Publisher: Pocket Books

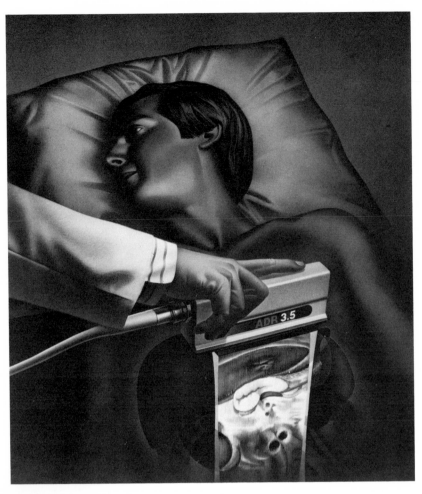

119
Advertising
Artist: **John Rush**
Art Director: Kenneth H. Lavey
Agency: Lavey/Wolff/Swift Inc.
Client: ADR Ultrasound

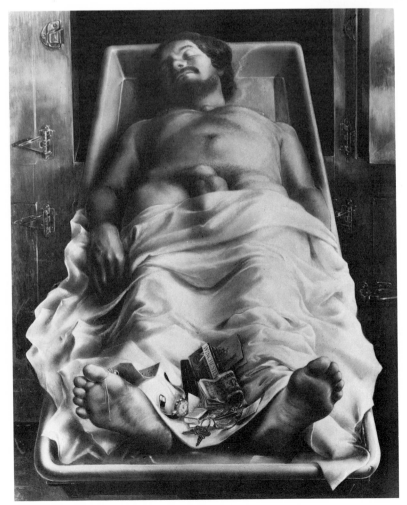

120
Editorial
Artist: **Kinuko Y. Craft**
Art Director: Rainer Wortmann
Publication: Playboy Deutschland

121
Advertising
Artist: **John Rush**
Art Director: Len Obatz
Agency: Wesson & Warhaftig
Client: Dupont

122
Book
Artist: **Allan Mardon**
Art Director: Tom VonDerLinn
Title: The Making of a Surgeon
Publisher: Reader's Digest

123
Book
Artist: **Jim Campbell**
Art Director: Tom VonDerLinn
Title: Arrowsmith
Publisher: Reader's Digest

124
Book
Artist: **Jim Campbell**
Art Director: Tom VonDerLinn
Title: Arrowsmith
Publisher: Reader's Digest

125
Book
Artist: **Jim Campbell**
Art Director: Tom VonDerLinn
Title: Arrowsmith
Publisher: Reader's Digest

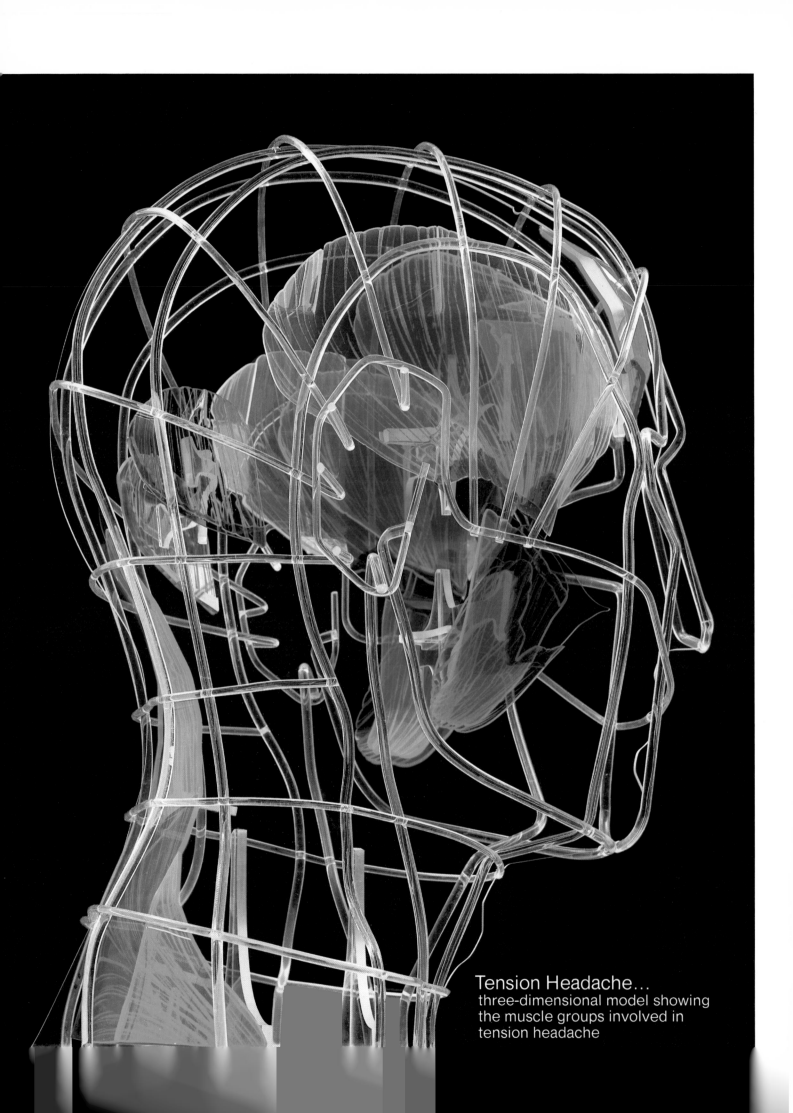

Tension Headache...
three-dimensional model showing
the muscle groups involved in
tension headache

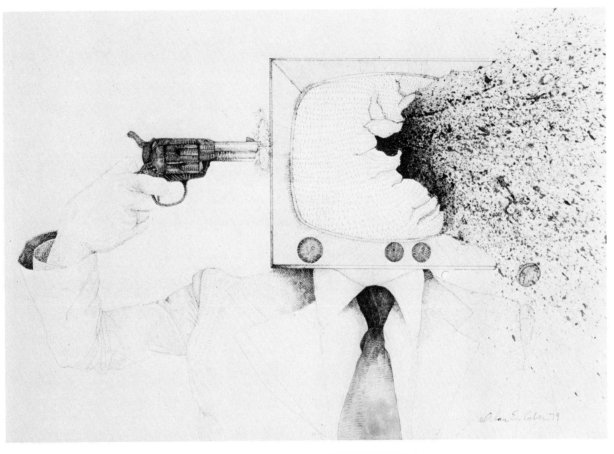

135
Editorial
Artist: **Alan E. Cober**
Art Director: Bob Post
Publication: Playboy Magazine

136
Institutional
Artist: **Alan E. Cober**
Art Director: Ethel Kessler Freid
Client: International Communication Agency

137
Advertising
Artist: **Larry Winborg**
Art Director: Larry Winborg

138
Book
Artist: **Herbert Tauss**
Art Director: Gordon Fisher
Title: Light in August
Publisher: Franklin Library

139
Institutional
Artist: **John M. Thompson**
Art Director: Scott Service
Client: Coors Beer

140
Advertising
Artist: **Everett Raymond Kinstler**
Art Director: Dean Krakel, Rich Muno
Client: National Cowboy Hall of Fame

141
Editorial
Artist: **David Griffin**
Art Director: Roger Pendleton
Publication: Texas Woman Magazine

144
Book
Artist: **Murray Tinkleman**
Art Director: Milton Charles
Title: Deerstalker
Publisher: Pocket Books

143
Book
Artist: **Murray Tinkleman**
Art Director: Milton Charles
Title: Lonestar Ranger
Publisher: Pocket Books

142
Advertising
Artist: **Bart Forbes**
Art Director: Jeannine White
Client: Cutter Bill Western World

145
Artist: **Murray Tinkelman**
Art Director: Milton Charles
Title: Arizona Clan
Publisher: Pocket Books

148
Book
Artist: **Walt Spitzmiller**
Art Director: David M. Seager
Title: Life on the Mississippi
Client: National Geographic Society

149
Book
Artist: **Roy Andersen**
Art Director: David M. Seager
Publisher: National Geographic Society

150
Advertising
Artist: **James McMullan**
Art Director: Paula Scher
Client: Columbia Records

147
Advertising
Artist: **Wilson McLean**
Art Director: Simon Bowden
Agency: Needham, Harper, Steers
Client: Union Carbide

151
Book
Artist: **Howard Rogers**
Art Director: Gordon Fisher
Title: Evidence of Love
Publisher: Franklin Library

152
Book
Artist: **Roger Kastel**
Art Director: Milton Charles
Title: Destiny's Children
Publisher: Pocket Books

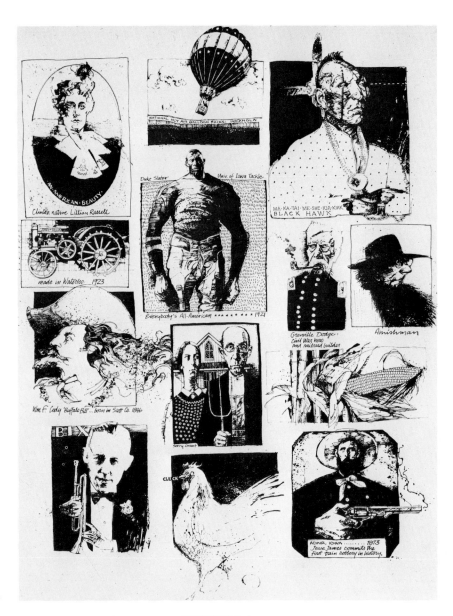

153
Institutional
Artist: **Gary Kelley**
Art Director: Gary Kelley
Client: Hellman Design Associates

154
Editorial
Artist: **Chris Duke**
Art Director: Chris Duke

156
Editorial
Artist: **Bob Crofut**
Art Director: Sal Lazarotti
Publication: Guideposts

157
Institutional
Artist: **Stan Miller**
Art Director: Stan Miller

155
Institutional
Artist: **Bob Crofut**
Art Director: Bob Crofut

158
Institutional
Artist: **Jack Unruh**
Art Director: Carl Lively
Client: Supron

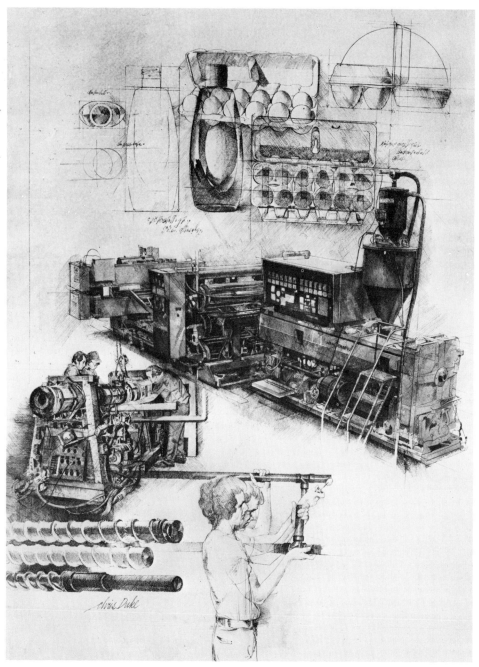

159
Institutional
Artist: **Chris Duke**
Art Director: Jack Hough
Agency: Jack Hough Assoc.
Client: Condec

160
Institutional
Artist: **David McCall Johnston**
Art Director: David McCall Johnston

161
TV
Artist: **Tim Boxell**
Art Director: Damon Rarey
Client: "Over Easy" KQED, Inc.

162
Institutional
Artist: **Thom Ricks**
Art Director: Thom Ricks
Agency: Konig Group
Client: Margaret Oates

163
Institutional
Artist: **Dickran Palulian**
Art Director: Steve Phillips
Agency: Steve Phillips Design
Client: Datamation

164
Institutional
Artist: **Kenneth Francis Dewey**
Art Director: Daniele Deverin
Client: Daniele Deverin

165
Institutional
Artist: **Robert M. Cunningham**
Art Director: Scott Samuel
Agency: Ogilvy & Mather/2
Client: New York University

166
Institutional
Artist: **Robert M. Cunningham**
Art Director: Scott Samuel
Agency: Ogilvy & Mather/2
Client: New York University

167
Institutional
Artist: **David B. McMacken**
Art Director: Karl Bornstien
Agency: Mirage Editions
Client: Tom Dean

168
Institutional
Artist: **Curtis G. Knapp**
Art Director: Curtis G. Knapp

169
Editorial
Artist: **Don Ivan Punchatz**
Art Director: Joe Brooks
Publication: Penthouse Magazine

170
Editorial
Artist: **William A. Motta**
Art Director: William A. Motta
Publication: Road & Track Magazine

171
Institutional
Artist: **Dick Lubey**
Art Director: Jack Matott
Agency: G M Dubois, Inc.
Client: Black & Decker

172
TV
Artist: **Gary Cooley**
Art Directors: Joe Minnella/Al Gay
Agency: W. B. Doner & Co.
Client: Taubman Co.
Production Company: Bajus-Jones Film Corp
Director: Don Bajus
Producer: Al Gay

173
Institutional
Artist: **Patrick Bailey**
Art Director: Tyler Smith
Agency: Tyler Smith Art Direction
Client: Foremost Lithographers

174
Institutional
Artist: **Scott Greer**
Art Director: Michael Richards
Client: Financial Aids & Scholarships
       University of Utah

175
Institutional
Artist: **Dick Lubey**
Art Director: Dick Lubey
Client: Dave Leveille

176
Book
Artist: **John Batchelor**
Art Director: Herbert Quarmby
Title: The Dreadnoughts
Publisher: Time-Life Books

177
Editorial
Artist: **Don Hedin**
Art Director: Don Hedin

178
Book
Artist: **Christopher Blossom**
Art Director: Len Leone
Title: The Cruel Sea
Publisher: Bantam Books Inc.

179
Advertising
Artist: **Arthur Shilstone**
Art Director: Robert Schulman
Client: NASA

180
Institutional
Artist: **Bill Heuer**
Art Director: Bill Heuer
Client: Maritz Motivation

181
Institutional
Artist: **Walter Einsel**
Art Director: Walter Einsel

182
Book
Artist: **Lou Feck**
Art Director: Len Leone
Title: City Wars
Publisher: Bantam Books

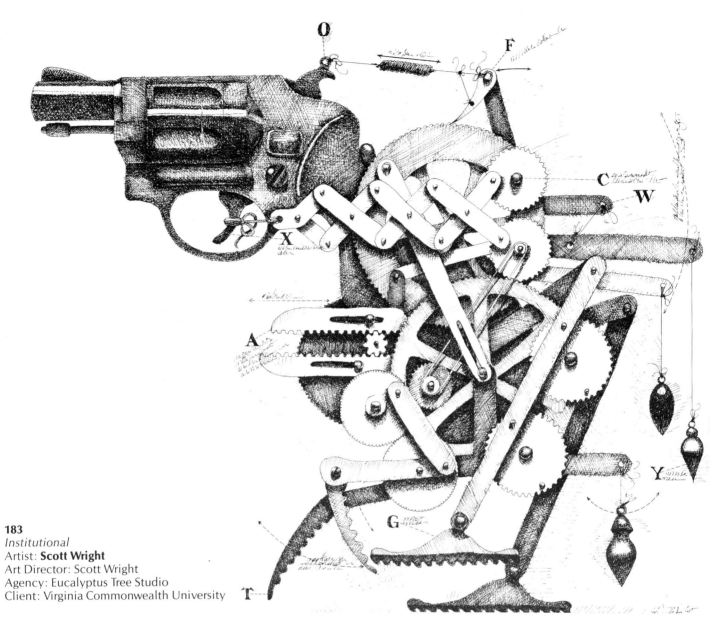

183
Institutional
Artist: **Scott Wright**
Art Director: Scott Wright
Agency: Eucalyptus Tree Studio
Client: Virginia Commonwealth University

184
Institutional
Artist: **Benjamin Eisenstat**
Art Director: B. Eisenstat

185
Book
Artist: **John Berkey**
Art Director: Gene Light
Title: Space Trek
Publisher: Warner Books

186
Advertising
Artist: **John Berkey**
Art Director: Ed Brodkin
Agency: Diener/Hauser/Bates Co. Inc.
Client: American International

187
Advertising
Artist: **Katheryn Holt**
Art Director: Katheryn Holt
Client: Paper Moon Graphics

188
Institutional
Artist: **John Berkey**
Art Director: Kerry O'Quinn
Publication: Future Magazine

189
Institutional
Artist: **Bob Dacey**
Art Director: Tycho Weil
Agency: Marquad & Roche
Client: Air Express International

190
Book
Artist: **Frank Wootton**
Art Director: Arnold C. Holeywell
Title: Knights of the Air
Publisher: Time-Life Books

191
Institutional
Artist: **Chris Duke**
Art Director: Jack Hough
Client: General Electric

192
Editorial
Artist: **Ken Dallison**
Art Director: Bud Loader
Publication: Ziff-Davis/"Flying" Magazine

193
Institutional
Artist: **Robert M. Cunningham**
Art Director: David G. Foote
Client: U.S. Postal Service
Gold Medal

194
Editorial
Artist: **Ken Dallison**
Art Director: Anthony J. Nelson
Publication: Car & Driver

195
Editorial
Artist: **Ellen Griesedieck**
Art Director: William A. Motta
Publication: Road & Track Magazine

196
Institutional
Artist: **Don Weller**
Art Director: Herb Gross
Agency: Smith & Hemmings
Client: Flying Tigers Airlines

197
Institutional
Artist: **Don Weller**
Art Director: Herb Gross
Agency: Smith & Hemmings
Client: Flying Tigers Airlines

WILSON McLEAN

198
Editorial
Artist: **Wilson McLean**
Art Director: Richard Gangel
Publication: Sports Illustrated

199
Institutional
Artists: **Lee & Mary Sievers**
Art Director: Lee Sievers

200
Institutional
Artists: **Lee & Mary Sievers**
Art Director: Lee Sievers

201
Institutional
Artists: **Lee & Mary Sievers**
Art Director: Lee Sievers
Client: Chas. Keeler Photography

202
Advertising
Artist: **Lou Myers**
Art Director: Paul Crifo
Agency: Diener/Hauser-Bates
Client: United Artists

203
Advertising
Artist: **Lou Myers**
Art Director: Burt Kleeger
Agency: J. Caroff Associates
Client: United Artists

204
Advertising
Artists: **Lee & Mary Sievers**
Art Director: Lee Sievers
Client: Twin City Dart Assoc.

206
Editorial
Artist: **Joe Isom**
Art Director: Dave Boss
Publication: Pro Magazine

207
Editorial
Artist: **Richard Waldrep**
Art Director: Greg Paul
Publication: Ohio Magazine

208
Editorial
Artist: **Mark Hess**
Art Director: Michael Brock/James Kiehle
Publication: Oui Magazine

205
Editorial
Artist: **Joe Isom**
Art Director: Dave Boss
Publication: Pro Magazine

209
Editorial
Artist: **Jon McIntosh**
Art Director: Ronn Campisi
Publication: Boston Globe

210
Institutional
Artist: **Cat Hnatov**
Art Director: Alan Gabay
Client: Crabwalk, Inc.

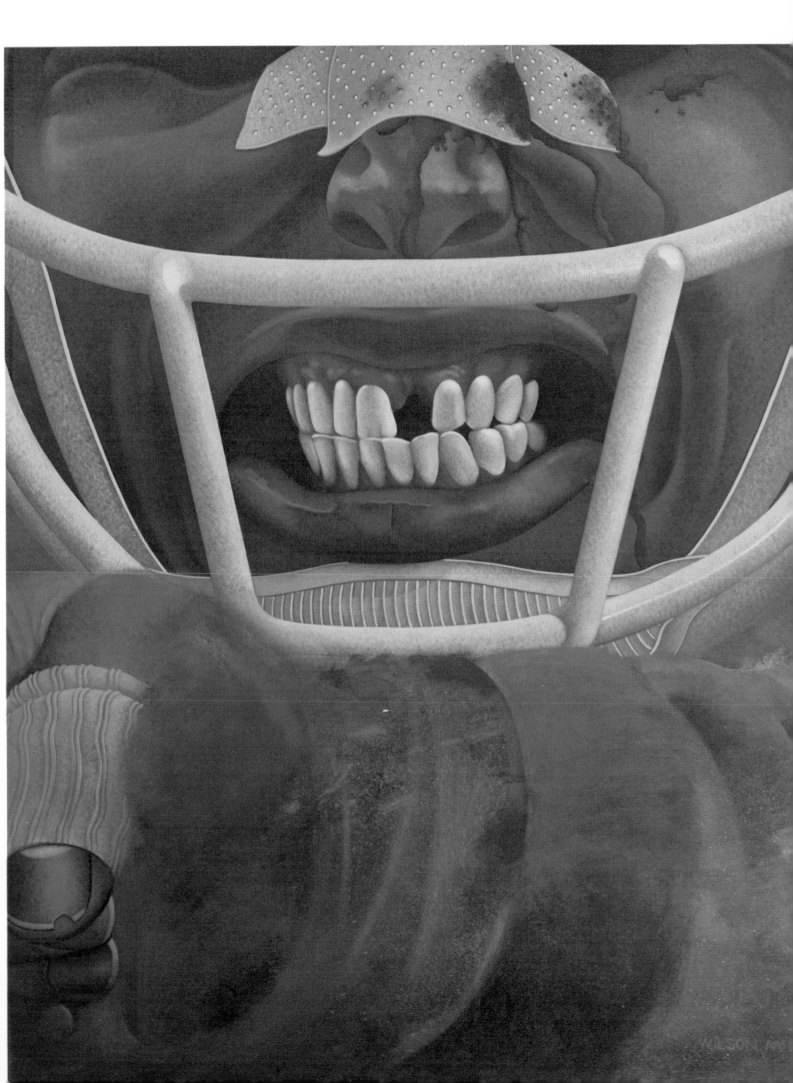

XIII Olympic Winter Games · Lake Placid · 1980

220
Advertising
Artist: **Robert M. Cunningham**
Art Director: Iska Rothovius
Client: New York Telephone, U.S. Olympic
       Committee & Lake Placid Olympic
       Organization Committee

221
Editorial
Artist: **David Boston**
Art Director: Fred Woodward
Publication: Memphis Magazine

222
Editorial
Artist: **Walt Spitzmiller**
Art Director: Richard Gangel
Publication: Sports Illustrated

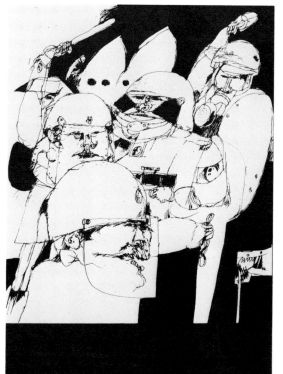

223
Institutional
Artist: **Salvador Bru**
Art Director: Ethel Kessler Freid
Client: International Communication Agency

224
Editorial
Artist: **David Grove**
Art Director: David Boss
Publication: NFL Properties Inc.

225
Editorial
Artist: **Joe Isom**
Art Director: Dave Boss
Publication: Pro Magazine

226
Institutional
Artist: **Debora A. Whitehouse**
Art Director: Don Dame
Client: Windemere Press
Award of Excellence

227
Institutional
Artist: **Carol Inouye**
Art Director: Carol Inouye

228
Editorial
Artist: **Ken Westphal**
Art Director: Jim Selzer
Publication: Star Magazine
Award of Excellence

229
Editorial
Artist: **John Robinette**
Art Director: Norman Oberlander
Publication: Swank Magazine
Most Outstanding Humor/Satire Illustration

230
Institutional
Artists: **Jane Del Villar & Bruce Brdar**
Art Director: Alan Gabay
Agency: Crabwalk, Inc.

231
Editorial
Artist: **Brad Holland**
Art Directors: Art Paul/Kerig Pope
Publication: Playboy Magazine

232
TV
Artist: **Jim Denney**
Art Director: Jim Denney
Client: WTAE-TV, American Diabetes Assoc.

233
Institutional
Artist: **Laura Cornell**
Art Director: Don Dame
Client: Windemere Press

234
TV
Artist: **Bill Dula**
Art Director: Lee Stausland
Client: NBC News

235
Advertising
Artist: **Bob Ziering**
Art Director: Susan Eckrote
Agency: Bergelt Advertising Inc.
Client: Schering Corp.

236
Advertising
Artist: **Paul M. Gleason**
Art Director: Paul M. Gleason

237
Editorial
Artist: **Ray Goodbread**
Art Director: Frank Devino
Publication: Omni Publications

238
Advertising
Artist: **Carl Heldt**
Art Director: Malice
Agency: Wehstein Advertising
Client: Wehstein Advertising

239
Editorial
Artist: **Malcolm T. Liepke**
Art Director: Phyllis Cayton
Publication: Sport Magazine
Norman Rockwell Award

240
Advertising
Artist: **Bernie Fuchs**
Art Director: Iska Rothovius
Client: New York Telephone
        U.S. Olympic Committee
        Lake Placid Olympic Organization
        Committee
Award of Excellence

241
Institutional
Artist: **Laurie Marks**
Art Director: John deCesare
Client: Illustrators' Workshop

242
Institutional
Artist: **Doug Johnson**
Art Director: Michael Hart
Agency: J. Walter Thompson
Client: Bausch & Lomb
Award of Excellence

243
Advertising
Artist: **Bob Heindel**
Art Director: Vince Maiello
Client: Playboy Book Club

244
Advertising
Artist: **Walter Rane**
Art Director: David Hankins

245
Book
Artist: **Bart Forbes**
Art Director: B. Martin Pedersen
Agency: Jonson, Pedersen, Hinrich &
         Shakery, Inc.
Publisher: Nautical Quarterly Inc.

246
Book
Artist: **Bill Elliott**
Art Director: Lidia Ferrara
Title: Streamers & Bucktails
Publisher: Alfred A. Knopf, Inc.

247
Institutional
Artist: **Robert Hanselmann**
Art Director: Robert Hanselmann
Client: Maritz Motivation

248
Editorial
Artist: **John Collier**
Art Director: Richard Gangel
Publication: Sports Illustrated

250
Institutional
Artist: **Fred W. Thomas**
Art Director: Fred W. Thomas

249
Editorial
Artist: **James McMullan**
Art Director: Carol Carson
Publication: Scholastic Magazines, Inc.

251
Institutional
Artist: **Rob Wood**
Art Director: Rob Wood
Agency: Stansbury, Ronsaville, Wood Inc.
Client: Cascio-Wood Inc.

252
Editorial
Artist: **Francis Golden**
Art Director: James Eisenman
Publication: Sports Afield Magazine

TOWN & COUNTRY's
health and beauty guide to
International Travel

253
Editorial
Artist: **Ronald Searle**
Art Director: Linda Stillman
Publication: Town & Country Magazine

254
Advertising
Artist: **Mary Ann Sullivan**
Art Director: Bill Dinkins
Agency: Lord, Sullivan & Yoder
Client: Railroad Savings & Loan

255
Institutional
Artist: **Christoher Magadini**
Art Director: Christopher Magadini

256
Institutional
Artist: **Christopher Magadini**
Art Director: Christopher Magadini

257
Institutional
Artist: **Joseph Ciardiello**
Art Director: Joseph Ciardiello
Client: Moonlight Press

258
Institutional
Artist: **John T. Burgoyne**
Art Director: Carol Ross
Agency: McKinney/New England
Client: Boston Ad Club

259
Book
Artist: **Bob Crofut**
Art Director: Bob Crofut

260
Institutional
Artist: **Julie Shearer**
Client: Sunrise Publications, Inc.

261
Editorial
Artist: **Mark Hess**
Art Director: Donald A. Adamec
Publication: Ladies' Home Journal

262
Book
Artist: **Jerry Pinkney**
Art Director: Jack Tauss
Title: Faulkner These Thirteen
Publisher: Franklin Library

263
Book
Artist: **Jerry Pinkney**
Art Director: Atha Tehon
Title: Tonweya and the Eagles
Publisher: The Dial Press

264
Book
Artist: **Joe Isom**
Art Director: Barbara Bertoli
Title: Hunters Horn
Publisher: Avon Books

265
Book
Artist: **Ted Lewin**
Art Director: Nick Calabrese
Title: Kola the Bear
Publisher: Reader's Digest General Books

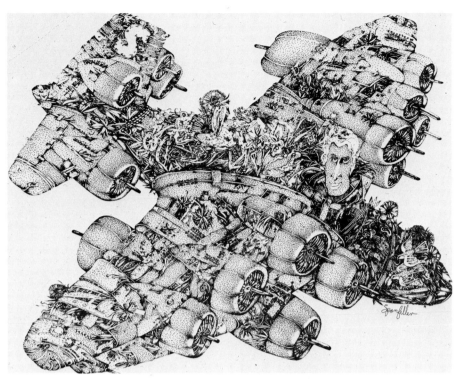

266
Editorial
Artist: **Jim Spanfeller**
Art Director: Herb Lubalin
Agency: Herb Lubalin Assoc.
Publication: U&lc

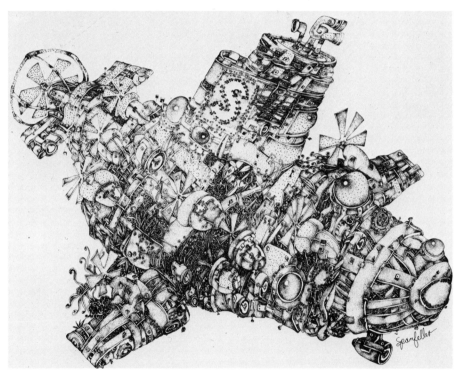

267
Editorial
Artist: **Jim Spanfeller**
Art Director: Herb Lubalin
Agency: Herb Lubalin Assoc.
Publication: U&lc

268
Institutional
Artist: **Sandy Huffaker**
Art Director: Sandy Huffaker

269
Institutional
Artist: **Jack Unruh**
Art Director: David M. Seager
Client: National Geographic Society

270
Editorial
Artist: **Oni**
Art Director: Victor J. Closi
Client: CBS Publications
Publication: Field & Stream

271
Editorial
Artist: **Ralph Steadman**
Art Director: Joe Brooks
Publication: Penthouse Magazine

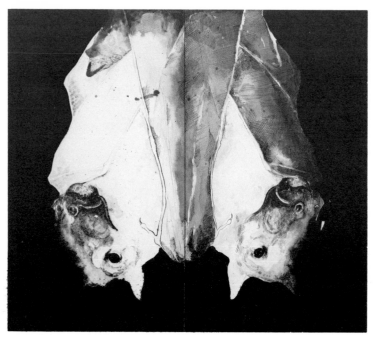

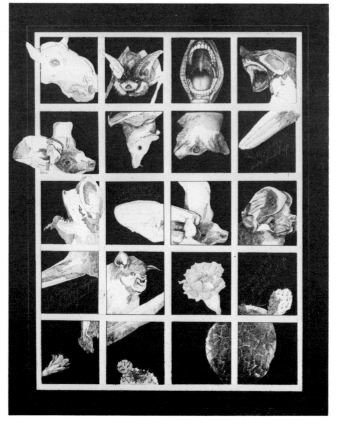

272
Institutional
Artist: **Sandra Filippucci**
Art Director: Sandra Filippucci
Client: Prehensile Pencil, Inc.

273
Institutional
Artist: **Sandra Filippucci**
Art Director: Sandra Filippucci
Client: Prehensile Pencil, Inc.

274
Book
Artist: **Alan E. Cober**
Art Director: Riki Levinson Meri Shardin
Publication: E.P. Dutton, Unicorn Books

275
Institutional
Artist: **Alan E. Cober**
Art Director: Carol Carson
Publisher: Scholastic Magazines

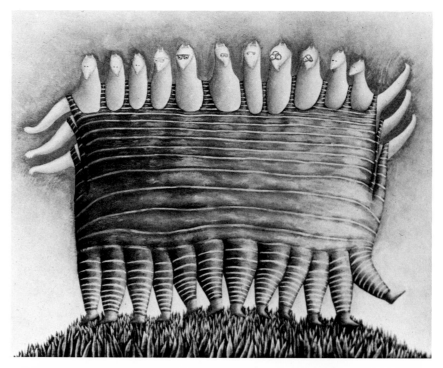

276
Institutional
Artist: **Rosalind Ivens**
Art Director: Rosalind Ivens

277
Book
Artist: **Tom Hall**
Art Director: William Gregory
Title: Strangers on a Train
Publisher: Reader's Digest

278
Editorial
Artist: **Marvin Mattelson**
Art Director: Milton Glaser
Publication: Esquire Magazine

279
TV
Artist: **Bill Davis**
Art Director: John Shrum
Agency: NBC Graphic Arts
Client: The Tonight Show

280
Book
Artist: **Robert J. Lee**
Art Director: Bill Martin, Jr.
Title: A Super Midnight Menu
Publisher: Holt, Rinehart, Winston

281
Advertising
Artist: **Paul Giovanopoulos**
Art Director: Paul Giovanopoulos
Client: Paul Giovanopoulos

282
Advertising
Artist: **Bart Forbes**
Art Director: Deborah Dalfovo
Agency: D'Arcy-MacManus & Masius
Client: Whirlpool Corporation

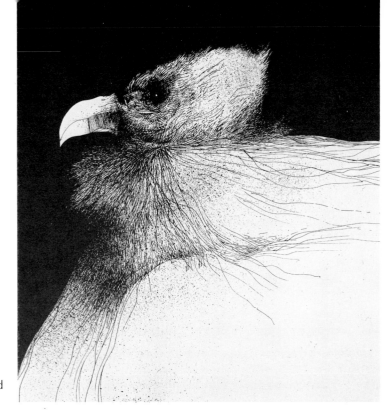

283
Advertising
Artist: **Michael David Brown**
Art Director: Ethel Kessler Freid
Client: U.S. Government

284
Editorial
Artist: **Bernie Fuchs**
Art Director: Richard Gangel
Publication: Sports Illustrated

285
Advertising
Artist: **Susan Jeffers**
Art Director: Atha Tehon
Client: The Dial Press

286
Book
Artist: **Renée Quintal Daily**
Art Director: Renée Quintal Daily

287
Book
Artist: **Leonard Baskin**
Art Director: Barbara G. Hennessy
Title: Hosie's Aviary
Publisher: The Viking Press, Inc.

288
Institutional
Artist: **Scott Reynolds**
Art Director: Scott Reynolds

289
Institutional
Artist: **Stan Miller**
Art Director: Stan Miller

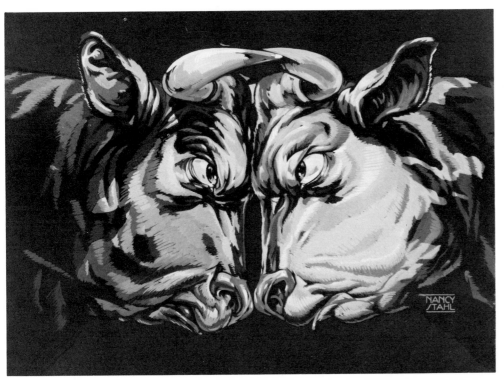

290
Editorial
Artist: **Nancy Stahl**
Art Director: J. C. Suares
Publication: New York Magazine

291
Advertising
Artist: **Teresa Fasolino**
Art Director: Milton Glaser
Agency: Milton Glaser Assocs.
Client: Grand Union Co.

292
Institutional
Artist: **Shelley Thornton**
Art Director: Carol Carson
Client: Scholastic Magazines, Inc.

293
Advertising
Artist: **Wally Neibart**
Art Director: Roger Raymor
Agency: Tailford Advertising
Client: Mach 1 International

294
TV
Artist: **Bob Peluce**
Art Director: Art Able
Director: Bob Kurtz
Producer: Jim Deasy
Agency: Kurtz & Friends
Client: Mug Root Beer
Award of Excellence

295
TV
Artist: **Bob Peluce**
Art Director: Art Able
Director: Bob Kurtz
Producer: Jim Deasy
Agency: Kurtz & Friends
Client: Mug Root Beer
Gold Medal

296
Editorial
Artist: **Dickran Palulian**
Art Director: Joe Brooks
Publication: Penthouse Magazine

297
Institutional
Artist: **Laurie Noble**
Art Director: Don Dame
Client: Windemere Press

298
Institutional
Artist: **Alton V. Langford**
Art Director: Alton V. Langford
Client: Current Inc.

299
Book
Artist: **Laura Cornell**
Art Director: Richard Laurent
Publisher: Encyclopaedia Britannica
Educational Corp.

300
Institutional
Artist: **Kirsten Soderlind**
Art Director: Steve Collier
Agency: Collier's Advertising Studio
Client: Oxy Chemical

301
Editorial
Artist: **Lemuel Line**
Art Director: Lemuel Line

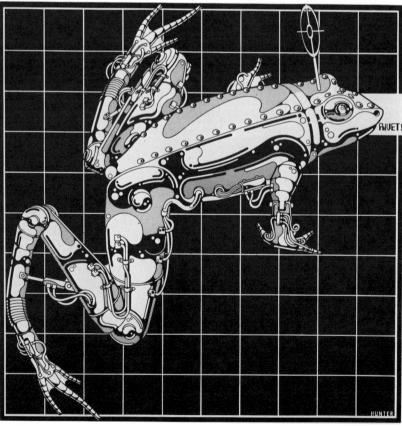

302
Institutional
Artist: **Stephen Hunter**
Art Director: Gary Kelley
Client: Hellman Design Associates

303
Advertising
Artist: **Scott Wright**
Art Director: Scott Wright
Agency: Eucalyptus Tree Studio

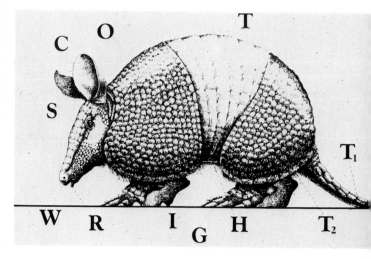

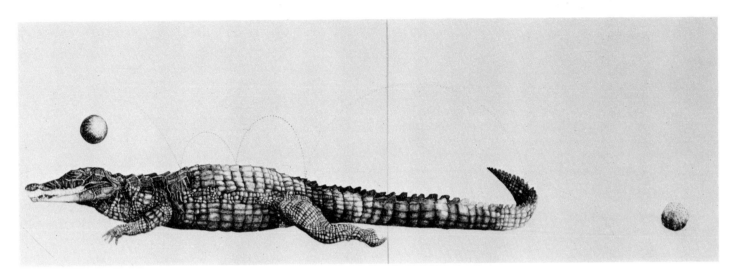

304
Book
Artist: **Alan E. Cober**
Art Directors: Riki Levinson, Meri Shardin
Publisher: E.P. Dutton, Unicorn Books

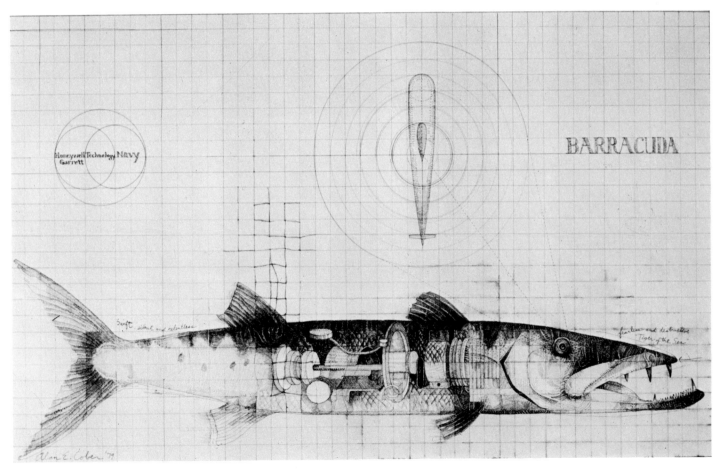

305
Advertising
Artist: **Alan E. Cober**
Art Director: Jim Canters
Client: Honeywell Corp.
Award of Excellence

The River Mississippi

315
Institutional
Artist: **Jerry Pinkney**
Art Director: Larry Borton
Client: Ashland Oil Inc.

316
Advertising
Artist: **Catherine Loeb**
Art Director: Nancy Donald
Client: CBS Records

317
TV
Artist: **Jacqui Morgan**
Art Director: Lou Del Pizo
Agency: Clyne Co. Adv.
Client: American Home Products

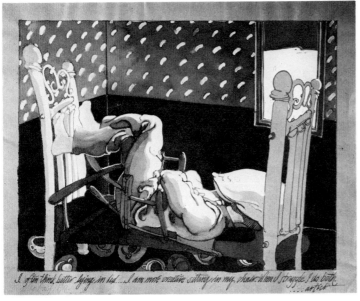

318
Institutional
Artist: **Michael Ng**
Art Director: Frank Hom
Agency: Epstein & Rayboy

319
Advertising
Artist: **Paul Lehr**
Art Director: Ed Harridsleff
Agency: Diener Hauser Bates
Client: Paramount Pictures

320
Institutional
Artist: **Wilson McLean**
Art Directors: David November/Don Lawson
Client: CBS Entertainment Press
        Information

321
Advertising
Artist: **Ed Lindlof**
Art Director: Ellie Malavis
Agency: Weekley & Penny, Inc.
Client: Friendswood Development Co.

322
Advertising
Artist: **Ed Lindlof**
Art Director: Al Gluth
Client: Harbour Martinique

323
Institutional
Artist: **Susan Sumichrast**
Art Director: Susan Sumichrast

324
Book
Artist: **Bill Davis**
Art Director: George Corsillo
Agency: Gribbitt!
Client: Casablanca Record & Film Works

325.
Editorial
Artist: **Barron Storey**
Art Director: Victor J. Closi
Publication: Field & Stream Magazine

326
Book
Artist: **Bob Dacey**
Art Director: Jack Tauss
Title: Other Voices—Other Rooms
Publisher: Franklin Library

327
Institutional
Artist: **Bettina Cato**
Art Director: Don Dame

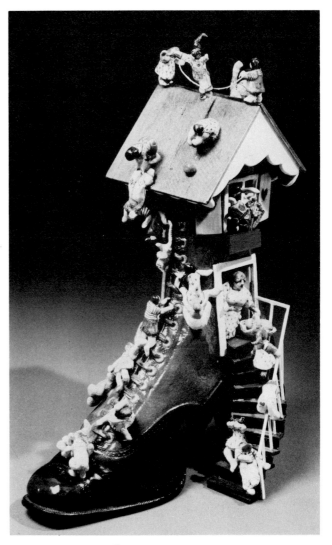

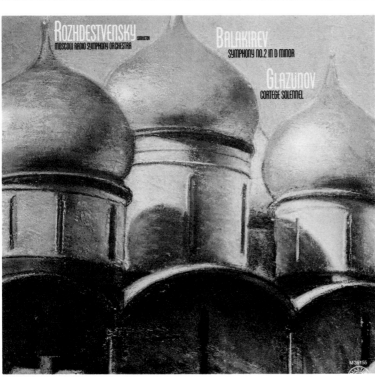

328
Advertising
Artist: **John Collier**
Art Director: Henrietta Condak
Client: CBS Records

329
Advertising
Artist: **Jill Weber**

June Reynard ©1979

330
Institutional
Artist: **June Reynard**
Art Director: June Reynard

331
Institutional
Artist: **Thomas B. Allen**
Art Director: Thomas B. Allen

332
Institutional
Artist: **Gregory Manchess**
Art Director: Duane Wood
Agency: Hellman Design Assoc.
Client: 3M Company

333
Book
Artist: **Richard Lovell**
Art Directors: Arnold C. Holeywell/Margaret Schreiber
Title: Vegetables—Good Cook Series
Publisher: Time-Life Books

334
Advertising
Artist: **James Barkley**
Art Director: James Barkley
Client: Superbrush Inc.

335
Institutional
Artist: **Sue Llewellyn**
Art Director: Sue Llewellyn
Client: Jack Strong

336
Institutional
Artist: **Sue Llewellyn**
Art Director: Sue Llewellyn
Client: Jack Strong

337
Institutional
Artist: **Robert P. Morello**
Art Director: Robert P. Morello

338
Editorial
Artist: **Richard Sparks**
Art Director: Joseph Connolly
Publication: Boy's Life Magazine

339
Advertising
Artist: **Brad Holland**
Art Director: Katherine Smith
Agency: Album Graphics
Client: Verve Records
Award of Excellence

340
Advertising
Artist: **Richard Sparks**
Art Director: Frank Wagner
Agency: Sudler & Hennessey, Inc.
Client: Endo Laboratories, Inc.

342
Institutional
Artist: **Martha Leugers**
Art Director: Martha Leugers
Agency: Cato Johnson, Inc.
Client: Summerfair Inc.

341
Advertising
Artist: **Milton Glaser**
Art Director: Milton Glaser
Agency: Milton Glaser, Inc.
Client: New York State Department
　　　of Commerce

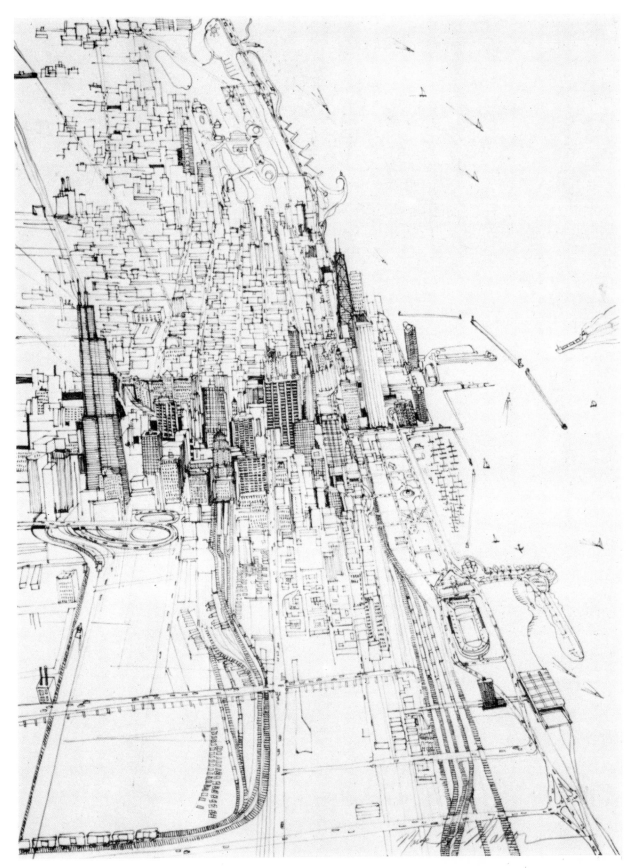

344
Institutional
Artist: **Mark McMahon**
Art Director: Nancy Rettinger
Agency: Haddon Advertising

343
Advertising
Artist: **Cheryl Cooper**
Art Director: Lionel Libson
Client: General Tire

345
Institutional
Artist: **Wendell Minor**
Art Director: Wendell Minor

346
Editorial
Artist: **Don Dixon**
Art Director: Cheh N. Low
Client: O'Quinn Studio

347
Advertising
Artist: **Jack Unruh**
Art Director: Lance Brown
Agency: The Richards Group
Client: Daon

348
Advertising
Artists: **Leo & Diane Dillon**
Art Director: Bob Gavin
Client: Caedmon Records

349
Institutional
Artist: **Albert Lorenz**
Art Director: Diana Graham
Agency: Diana Graham, Graphic Design
Client: Williamson, Pickett, Gross Real Estate

350
Advertising
Artist: **Cheryl Cooper**
Art Director: Lionel Libson
Client: General Tire

351
Institutional
Artist: **Thomas B. Allen**
Art Director: Thomas B. Allen

352
TV
Artist: **Gary Cooley**
Art Directors: Joe Minella/Al Gay
Agency: W.B. Doner & Co.
Client: Pillsbury
Production Company: Zanders
Animation Parlour
Director: Jack Zander
Producer: Al Gay

353
Editorial
Artist: **Emanuel Schongut**
Art Director: Seymour Chwast/Richard Mantel
Agency: Push Pin Studios, Inc.
Client: Push Pin Graphic

354
Editorial
Artist: **Thomas B. Allen**
Art Director: Milton Glaser
Publication: Esquire Magazine

355
Editorial
Artist: **Ignacio Gomez**
Art Director: Michael Brock
Publication: Oui Magazine

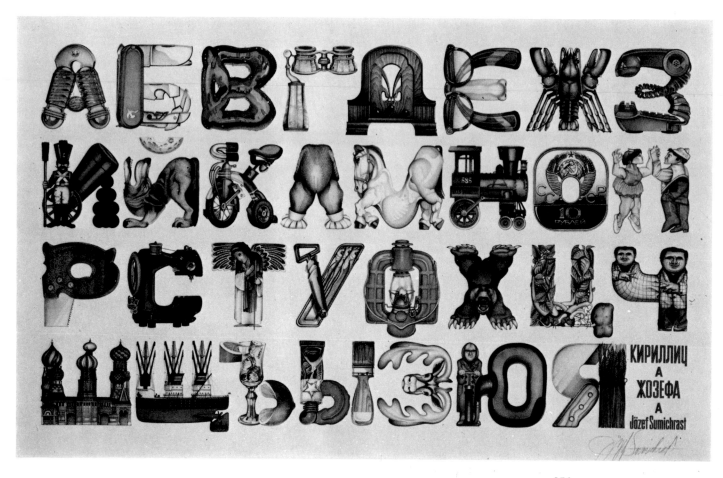

356
Institutional
Artist: **Jözef Sumichrast**
Art Director: Jözef Sumichrast

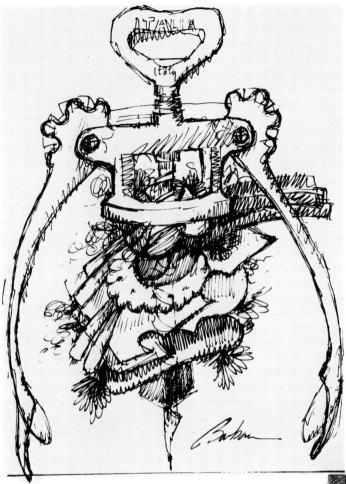

365
Institutional
Artist: **Geoffrey Moss**
Art Director: Ethel Kessler Freid
Client: International Communication Agency

364
Institutional
Artist: **Barbara Redmond**
Art Directors: Barbara Redmond/Patrick Redmond
Client: Barbara & Patrick Redmond Design

366
Editorial
Artist: **Steve Brodner**
Art Director: Steve Brodner
Publication: The New York Illustrated News

367
Editorial
Artist: **Louis Escobedo**
Art Director: Louis Escobedo
Client: KTXQ FM Station
Gold Medal

368
Advertising
Artist: **Paul Davis**
Art Director: Susan Lyster
Agency: McCaffrey & McCall
Client: Exxon Corp.

369
Advertising
Artist: **Edwin Herder**
Art Director: Dick Smith
Client: RCA Records

370
Book
Artist: **David Grove**
Art Director: John Van Zwienen
Title: Sharky's Machine
Publisher: Dell Publishing Co. Inc.
Most Outstanding Paperback Cover

371
Institutional
Artist: **Ted Fox**
Art Director: Ted Fox
Client: Maritz Motivation

372
Institutional
Artist: **Peter Lloyd**
Art Director: Tom Clemente
Agency: Newspaper Advertising Bureau
Client: Member Newspapers

373
Advertising
Artist: **Gary Meyer**
Art Director: Bill Wallen
Client: Thought Factory

374
Advertising
Artist: **Gary Meyer**
Art Director: Tony Lane
Client: CBS Records

375
Advertising
Artist: **Kenneth Francis Dewey**
Art Director: Maxeen Smart
Client: CBS Records

376
Institutional
Artist: **Dennis Ziemienski**
Art Director: Dennis Ziemienski
Client: Paper Moon Graphics

377
Editorial
Artist: **Jeff Cummins**
Art Directors: Michael Brock/Geo. Kenton
Publication: Oui Magazine

378
Advertising
Artist: **David B. McMacken**
Art Director: Dan Perri
Agency: Perri Graphics
Client: Steven Spielberg

379
Advertising
Artist: **Carol Inouye**
Art Director: Katrinka Blickle
Client: Arista Records

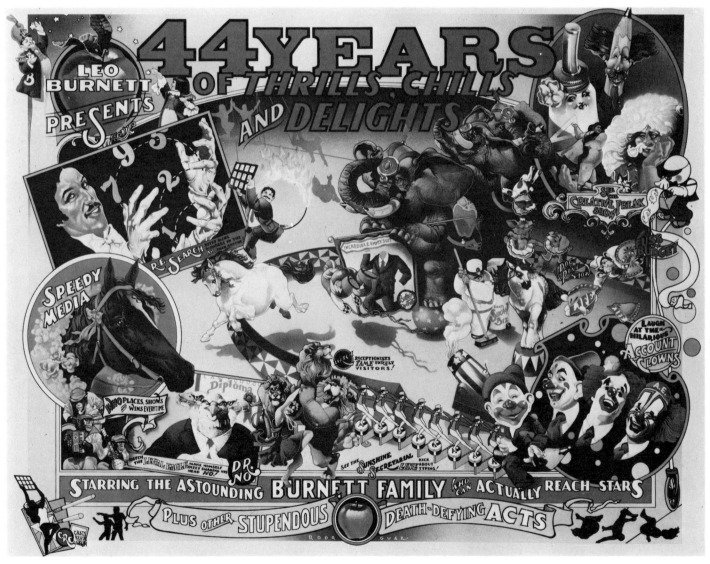

380
Institutional
Artist: **Robert B. Rodriguez**
Art Director: Bob Andrus
Agency: Leo Burnett Advertising
Client: Leo Burnett

381
Editorial
Artist: **John Berkey**
Art Director: Jerry Alten
Publication: TV Guide

382
TV
Artist: **Skip Ishii**
Art Director: Skip Ishii
Client: Seiko
Production Company: Skip
Ishii Productions, Inc.
Director: Wayne Kimbell
Producer: Skip Ishii

383
Book
Artist: **Doug Johnson**
Art Director: Bruce Hall
Title: The Story of Stevie Wonder
Publisher: Dell Publishing Co.

384
Advertising
Artist: **Bob Peak**
Art Director: Don Smolen
Agency: Smolen Smith & Connolly
Client: Warner Bros.

385
Advertising
Artist: **Shusei Nagaoka**
Art Director: Tony Lane
Client: CBS Records

386
Advertising
Artist: **Bob Peak**
Art Director: Don Smolen
Agency: Smolen Smith & Connolly
Client: United Artists

387
Advertising
Artist: **Bob Peak**
Art Director: Don Smolen
Agency: Smolen Smith & Connolly
Client: United Artists

388
Editorial
Artist: **Brad Holland**
Art Director: Pamela Vassil
Publication: The New York Times

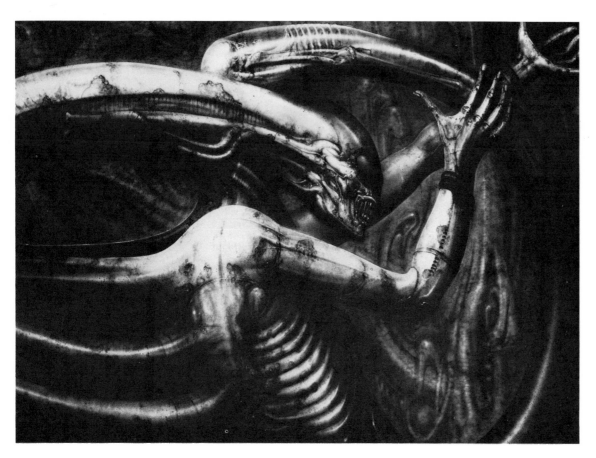

389
Editorial
Artist: **H. R. Giger**
Art Director: Frank Devino
Publication: Omni Publications

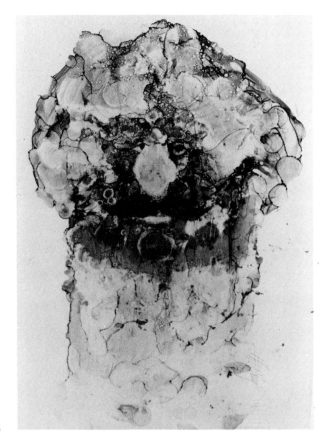

390
Advertising
Artist: **Howard Utley**
Art Director: Howard Utley
Agency: Utley/Schweizer Advertising

391
Advertising
Artist: **Jean-Marie Troillard**
Art Director: Reid Rosefelt
Client: New Yorker Films

392
Institutional
Artist: **Gary Kelley**
Art Director: Gary Kelley
Client: Hellman Design Associates

393
Editorial
Artist: **Stanley Meltzoff**
Art Director: Richard Gangel
Publication: Sports Illustrated

394
Advertising
Artist: **Robert Hickson**
Art Directors: Douglas Boyd,
                Scott. A. Mednick
Agency: Douglas Boyd Design & Marketing
Client: McGaw Laboratories

404
Institutional
Artist: **Frank A. Steiner**
Art Director: The Illustrators Workshop
Client: The Illustrators Workshop

405
Book
Artist: **David Grove**
Art Director: Len Leone
Title: Portnoy's Complaint
Publisher: Bantam Books, Inc.

406
Editorial
Artist: **Mara McAfee**
Art Director: Peter Kleinman
Publication: National Lampoon

407
Editorial
Artist: **Carol Wald**
Art Director: Jessica Weber
Publication: Food & Wine Magazine

408
Advertising
Artist: **Wayne McLoughlin**
Art Director: Wayne McLoughlin
Award of Excellence

409
Book
Artist: **Mitchell Hooks**
Art Director: Jack Tauss
Title: Tales from the East and West
Publisher: Franklin Library

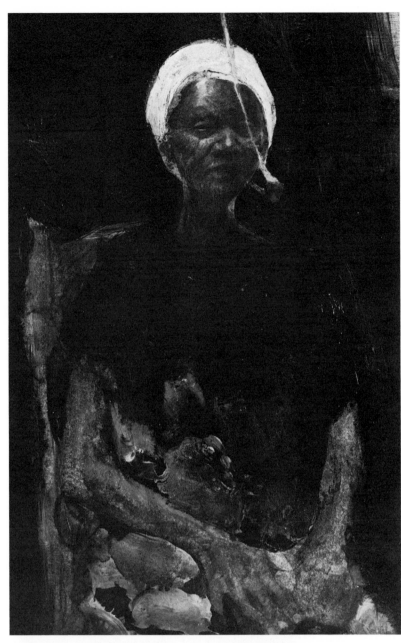

426
Book
Artist: **Herbert Tauss**
Art Director: Gordon Fisher
Title: Light in August
Publisher: Franklin Library
Most Outstanding Black and White Illustration

427
Book
Artist: **Rick McCollum**
Art Director: William Gregory
Title: Payment Deferred
Publisher: Reader's Digest

428
Institutional
Artist: **Sandy Huffaker**
Art Director: Sandy Huffaker

429
Advertising
Artist: **Gary Ruddell**
Art Director: Gary Ruddell

430
Advertising
Artist: **Charles Santore**
Art Director: Charles Santore
Client: Phoenix Theatre

431
Institutional
Artist: **Debbie Kuhn**
Art Director: Sky Hiers
Agency: Robertson Agency
Client: Variety Clubs International

432
Advertising
Artist: **Isadore Seltzer**
Art Director: Vince Marrapodi
Client: CBS Records

433
Advertising
Artist: **Chuck Wilkinson**
Art Director: Melonie Roher
Agency: Anthony Russell, Inc.
Client: Mobil Corp.

434
Institutional
Artist: **Lucy Gould**
Art Director: Lucy Gould

435
Advertising
Artist: **Christine Nasser**
Art Director: Henry Vizcarra
Client: Gribbitt!

436
Book
Artist: **Linda Fennimore**
Art Director: Linda Fennimore

437
Institutional
Artist: **Scott Greer**
Art Director: Michael Richards
Client: Division of Continuing Education
        University of Utah

438
Editorial
Artist: **John Collier**
Art Director: Maxine Davidowitz
Publication: Redbook Magazine

439
Advertising
Artist: **Ken Thompson**
Art Director: Ken Thompson
Agency: 2010 Advertising, Inc.

440
Advertising
Artist: **Peter M. Fiore**
Art Director: Ed Werth
Client: Literary Guild

441
Institutional
Artist: **Peter M. Fiore**
Art Director: Peter M. Fiore

442
Editorial
Artist: **Alex Gnidziejko**
Art Director: Modesto Torre
Publication: McCall's Magazine

443
Institutional
Artist: **Peter Cox**
Art Director: Peter Cox

444
TV
Artist: **Jane Sterrett**
Art Director: Jane Sterrett

454
Editorial
Artist: **Jim Spanfeller**
Art Director: Herb Lubalin
Agency: Herb Lubalin Assoc.
Publication: U&lc

455
Advertising
Artist: **Jim Spanfeller**
Art Director: Joel Fuller
Agency: K.S.W. & G.
Client: Ziff Davis Publications
Psychology Today Magazine

456
Advertising
Artist: **Sharka Glet**
Art Director: Sharka Glet

457
Institutional
Artist: **James Barkley**
Art Director: James Barkley
Client: Stogo Bernstein & Andriulli Inc.

458
Advertising
Artist: **Howard Utley**
Art Director: Howard Utley
Agency: Utley/Schweizer Advertising

459
Institutional
Artist: **Susan M. Blubaugh**
Art Director: Susan M. Blubaugh
Client: Susan M. Blubaugh

460
Institutional
Artist: **B. J. Johnson**
Art Director: B. J. Johnson

461
Editorial
Artist: **Steve Karchin**
Art Director: Salvatore Lazzarotti
Publication: Guideposts

462
Editorial
Artist: **Herbert Tauss**
Art Director: Salvatore Lazzarotti
Publication: Guideposts

463
Institutional
Artist: **Laura Cornell**
Art Director: Don Dame
Client: Windemere Press

464
Editorial
Artist: **Chris Duke**
Art Director: Chris Duke

473
TV
Artist: **Roy Ruan**
Art Director: Beverly Littlewood
Client: NBC-TV
Gold Medal

474
Institutional
Artist: **Norm Walker**
Art Director: W. B. Crabb
Client: W. B. Crabb

475
Book
Artist: **Bernie Fuchs**
Art Director: William Gregory
Title: Words by Heart
Publisher: Reader's Digest
Gold Medal

Hartford
Ballet
presents
The
Nutcracker

December
15-18

Bushnell
Hall

For tickets
call
246-6807

Thanks to United Technologies for this message

476
Advertising
Artist: **Ivan Chermayeff**
Art Director: Ivan Chermayeff
Agency: Chermayeff & Geismar
Client: United Technologies

477
Institutional
Artist: **Ivan Chermayeff**
Art Director: Mickey Tender
Client: U.S. Army

478
Book
Artist: **Mitchell Hooks**
Art Director: Jack Tauss
Title: Tales from the East and West
Publisher: Franklin Library

479
Book
Artist: **Bernie Fuchs**
Art Director: William Gregory
Title: Words by Heart
Publisher: Reader's Digest

480
Book
Artist: **Bernie Fuchs**
Art Director: William Gregory
Title: Words by Heart
Publisher: Reader's Digest

481
Book
Artist: **Bernie Fuchs**
Art Director: William Gregory
Title: Words by Heart
Publisher: Reader's Digest
Award of Excellence

482
Book
Artist: **Bernie Fuchs**
Art Director: Jack Tauss
Publisher: Franklin Library

483
Book
Artist: **Barbara Fox**
Art Director: Jack Tauss
Title: The Great Gatsby
Publisher: The Franklin Library

484
Book
Artist: **George H. Jones**
Art Director: Milt Charles
Title: The Fixer
Publisher: Pocket Books

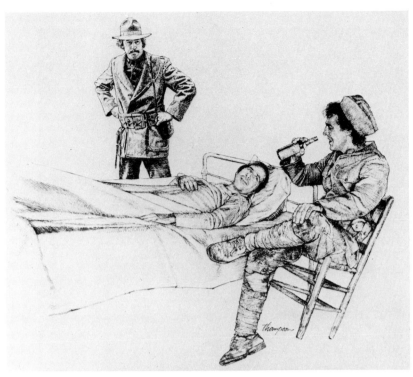

485
Editorial
Artist: **John M. Thompson**
Art Directors: Milton Glaser/Margery Peters
Publication: Esquire Magazine

486
Institutional
Artist: **Max Ginsburg**
Art Director: Max Ginsburg
Client: Gallery 306

487
Advertising
Artist: **Fred Otnes**
Art Director: Don Smolen
Client: United Artists

488
Advertising
Artist: **Ted CoConis**
Art Director: Burt Kleeger
Client: United Artists

489
Book
Artist: **Rick McCollum**
Art Director: Jim Plumeri
Client: New American Library

490
Institutional
Artist: **Jill Bossert**
Art Director: Jill Bossert
Client: R.S.V.P.

491
Institutional
Artist: **Bente Norgaard Adler**
Art Director: Bente Norgaard Adler
Agency: Adler-Schwartz Graphics, Inc.
Client: Adler-Schwartz Graphics, Inc.

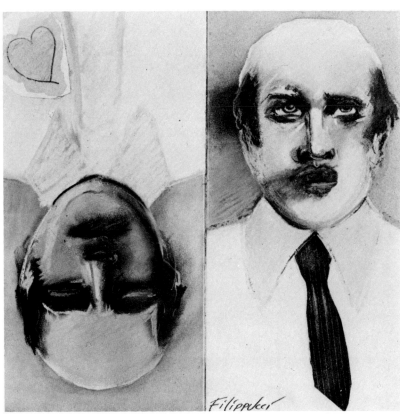

492
Editorial
Artist: **Sandra Filippucci**
Art Director: Tina Adamek
Publication: McGraw-Hill, Inc—
　　　　　　Postgraduate Medicine

493
Book
Artist: **Kenneth Francis Dewey**
Art Director: Jack Tauss
Title: James Joyce: Ulysses
Publisher: Franklin Library

494
Advertising
Artist: **Bob Heindel**
Art Director: Vince Maiello
Client: Playboy Book Club

495
Book
Artist: **Kenneth Francis Dewey**
Art Director: Jack Tauss
Title: Ulysses
Publisher: Franklin Library

496
Book
Artist: **Kenneth Francis Dewey**
Art Director: Jack Tauss
Title: James Joyce: Ulysses
Publisher: Franklin Library

497
Editorial
Artist: **Gregory E. Voth**
Art Director: Gregory E. Voth
Publication: Leisure Publishing

498
Advertising
Artist: **Thomas A. Woodruff**
Art Director: Thomas A. Woodruff

500
Advertising
Artist: **Charles Santore**
Art Director: Charles Santore
Client: Phoenix Theatre

501
Editorial
Artist: **Keith Batcheller**
Art Director: James Guerard
Agency: Hinsche, Kay & Associates
Client: Fluor Corp.

502
Book
Artist: **Jack Endewelt**
Art Director: Soren Noring
Title: A Theater of War
Publisher: The Reader's Digest

504
Institutional
Artist: **Tim Bowers**
Art Director: Frank Hoffelt
Agency: Wanamakers Ad Art Inc.
Client: Columbus College of Art & Design

503
Institutional
Artist: **Ellen Rixford**
Art Director: Marilyn Hoffner
Client: Cooper Union

505
Editorial
Artist: **Gottfried Helnwein**
Art Director: Frank Devino
Publication: Omni Publications

507
Advertising
Artist: **Brad Holland**
Art Director: Brad Holland
Client: Books & Co.

506
Editorial
Artist: **Brad Holland**
Art Directors: Art Paul/Kerig Pope
Publication: Playboy Magazine

508
Editorial
Artist: **Brad Holland**
Art Director: David Schniederman
Publication: The Village Voice

509
Institutional
Artist: **Jan Sawka**
Art Director: Lynn Hollyn
Client: M.U.S.E.

510
Book
Artist: **Chet Jezierski**
Art Director: Barbara Bertoli
Title: The Yemenite Girl
Publisher: Avon Books

511
Book
Artist: **Ted Lewin**
Art Director: Nick Calabrese
Title: Jumper: Life of a Siberian Horse
Publisher: Reader's Digest General Books

512
Book
Artist: **David Blossom**
Art Director: Marion Davis
Title: The Tightrope Walker
Publisher: Reader's Digest Condensed Books

513
Editorial
Artist: **Louis S. Glanzman**
Art Director: Howard Paine
Publication: National Geographic Magazine

514
Editorial
Artist: **Stephen Rybka**
Art Director: Pelayia Limbos
Publication: The Rotarian Magazine

515
Book
Artist: **Dick Brown**
Art Director: Gordon Fisher
Title: The Reivers
Publisher: Franklin Library

516
Editorial
Artist: **Marvin Mattelson**
Art Director: Ron Campbell
Publication: Fortune Magazine
Award of Excellence

517
Book
Artist: **Rick McCollum**
Art Director: William Gregory
Title: Payment Deferred
Publisher: Reader's Digest

518
Book
Artist: **David Grove**
Art Director: Len Leone
Title: Call for the Dead
Publisher: Bantam Books, Inc.

519
Book
Artist: **Lou Glanzman**
Art Director: Len Leone
Title: The Brotherhood of the Grape
Publisher: Bantam Books, Inc.

520
Book
Artist: **Mark Bellerose**
Art Director: Jack Tauss
Title: Dubin's Lives
Publisher: The Franklin Library

521
Artist: **Mark Bellerose**
Art Director: Jack Tauss
Title: Dubin's Lives
Publisher: The Franklin Library

522
Editorial
Artist: **Bob Dacey**
Art Director: Joe Connolly
Publication: Boy's Life Magazine

523
Book
Artist: **Bob Dacey**
Art Director: Jack Tauss
Title: Other Voices—Other Rooms
Publisher: The Franklin Library

524
Book
Artist: **Mitchell Hooks**
Art Director: Jack Tauss
Title: Young Lonigan
Publisher: Franklin Library

525
Book
Artist: **Michael Dudash**
Art Director: Bruce Hall
Title: Man Without a Face
Publisher: Dell Publishing

526
Book
Artist: **Don Maitz**
Art Director: Milton Charles
Title: Road to Corlay
Publisher: Pocket Books
Award of Excellence

527
Book
Artist: **Brian Froud**
Art Director: David Larkin
Title: Faeries
Publisher: Bantam Books, Inc.
Award of Excellence

528
Institutional
Artist: **Carol Inouye**
Art Director: Murlin Marsh
Client: NBC-TV

529
Institutional
Artist: **Jerry Pinkney**
Art Director: Edward Cook
Agency: D'Arcy MacManus & Masius
Client: Budweiser

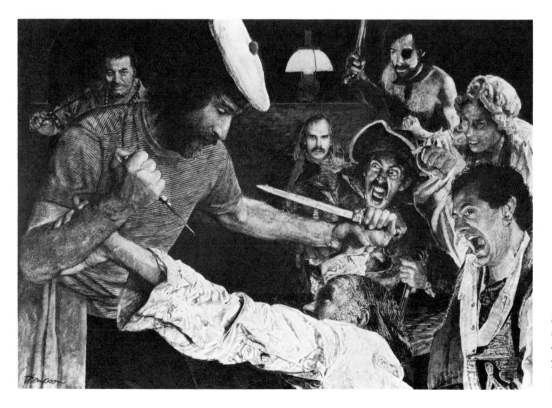

530
Book
Artist: **John M. Thompson**
Art Director: Gordon Fisher
Title: Count of Monte Cristo
Publisher: Franklin Library

531
Book
Artist: **Ben F. Stahl**
Art Director: Soren Noring
Title: To Build a Castle
Publisher: Reader's Digest

532
Institutional
Artist: **Victor Valla**
Art Director: Victor Valla
Client: Barnstone Gallery

533
Advertising
Artist: **Linda Gist**
Art Director: Elmer Pizzi
Agency: Gray & Rogers
Client: Weyerhaeuser Paper Co.

534
Institutional
Artist: **Heather Cooper**
Art Director: Lou Dorfsman
Client: CBS/ Broadcast Group
International Design Conference
Aspen

535
Institutional
Artist: **Kathy Krantz**
Art Director: Kathy Krantz

536
Book
Artist: **Bob Pepper**
Art Director: Lynn Hollyn
Title: Gallows Wedding
Publisher: Coward, McCann, Geoghegan

537
Book
Artists: **Leo & Diane Dillon**
Art Director: Lynn Hollyn
Title: The Goddess
Publisher: Coward, McCann & Geoghegan

538
Book
Artists: **Leo & Diane Dillon**
Art Director: John Granditsz
Title: Cricket Woman
Publication: Cricket Magazine

539
Advertising
Artist: **John Alcorn**
Art Director: Henrietta Condak
Client: CBS Records

540
Institutional
Artist: **David E. Levine**
Art Director: Elton R. Robinson
Client: Exxon Corporation

541
Book
Artist: **John M. Thompson**
Art Director: Gordon Fisher
Title: Madame duBarry
Publisher: Franklin Library
Award of Excellence

542
Editorial
Artist: **Donald Roller Wilson**
Art Director: Frank Devino
Publication: Omni Publications

543
Editorial
Artist: **Stan Hunter**
Art Director: Jerry Alten
Publication: TV Guide

544
Book
Artist: **Stan Hunter**
Art Director: Tom Vonderlinn
Title: The Cry & the Covenant
Publisher: Reader's Digest

545
Book
Artist: **Roger Kastel**
Art Director: Milton Charles
Title: Glendower Legacy
Publisher: Pocket Books

546
Institutional
Artist: **William Ersland**
Art Director: William Ersland
Client: Hellman Design

547
Advertising
Artist: **Doug Johnson**
Art Director: Gerry Diebart
Client: Schenley Imports

548
Book
Artist: **Herbert Tauss**
Art Director: George Cornell
Title: Wolf of Masada
Publisher: Avon Books

549
Book
Artist: **Tony Chen**
Art Director: Linda Zuckerman
Publisher: Viking Press, Inc.

550
Book
Artist: **Louis Glanzman**
Art Director: Len Leone
Publisher: Bantam Books, Inc.

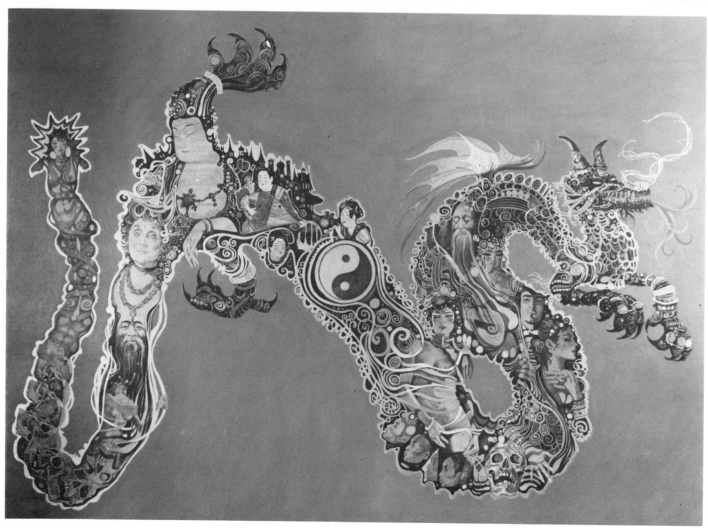

551
Book
Artist: **Ted CoConis**
Art Director: Dale Phillips
Title: Dynasty
Publisher: Fawcett Publications

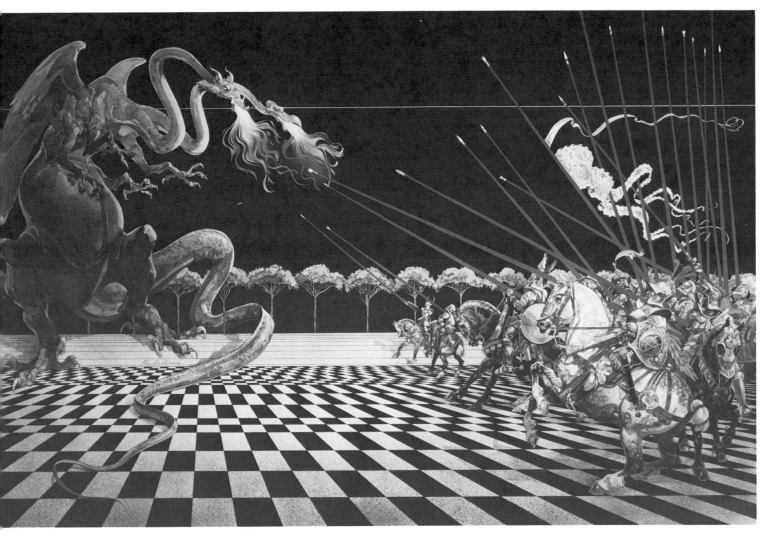

552
Book
Artist: **Roy Andersen**
Art Director: Ian Summers
Agency: Summers Productions

553
Institutional
Artist: **Charles Santore**
Art Director: Elmer Pizzi
Agency: Gray & Rogers
Client: Hunt Manufacturing Co.

554
TV
Artist: **Bill Davis**
Art Director: John Shrum
Agency: NBC Graphic Arts
Client: The Tonight Show

555
TV
Artist: **Bill Davis**
Art Director: John Shrum
Agency: NBC Graphic Arts
Client: The Tonight Show

556
Advertising
Artist: **Brenda Pepper**
Art Director: Dennis Barnett
Client: Random House Student Book Club

557
Book
Artist: **Frederic Marvin**
Art Director: Frank Kozelek
Title: Mistress Masham's Repose
Publisher: Berkley Publishing Corp.

558
Book
Artist: **Margot Tomes**
Art Director: Diane Stanley
Title: The Sorcerer's Apprentice
Publisher: Coward, McCann & Geoghegan

Inside this book
you'll meet...
abbey lubbers (devils who
live in monasteries, feasting
in cellars and tempting
the monks),
banshees (Celtic prophets of death),
boggarts (mischievous brownies
who plague households),
and more, guided by the enchanting
folklorist Katharine Briggs,
who "probably knows more
about hobgoblins, brownies,
and bogies than anyone
else now living"
(Alison Lurie).

It's a who's who of
the most wondrous sort!

Abbey Lubbers, Banshees & Boggarts

Katharine Briggs

Abbey
Lubbers,
Banshees &
Boggarts

An Illustrated
Encyclopedia of Fairies
Katharine
Briggs

Illustrated by
Yvonne Gilbert

Pantheon

0-394-50806-8

559
Book
Artist: **Yvonne Gilbert**
Art Director: Louise Fili
Title: Abbey Lubbers, Banshees & Boggart
Publisher: Pantheon Books

560
Editorial
Artist: **Tom Newsom**
Art Director: Harriet Greaney
Publication: Gift Digest Magazine

561
Institutional
Artist: **Louis Escobedo**
Art Director: Louis Escobedo
Client: Louis Escobedo

562
Institutional
Artist: **Sarah Hewitt**
Art Director: Sarah Hewitt
Agency: Flemister & Burkhardt
Client: Alliance Theatre

563
Book
Artist: **Charles Mikolaycak**
Art Director: Lucy Bitzer
Title: The Suprising Things Maui Did
Publisher: Four Winds Press

564
TV
Artist: **Catherine Parker Bubert**
Art Director: Catherine Parker Bubert
Title: The Ostrich
Client: Maryland Center for Public Broadcasting
Award of Excellence

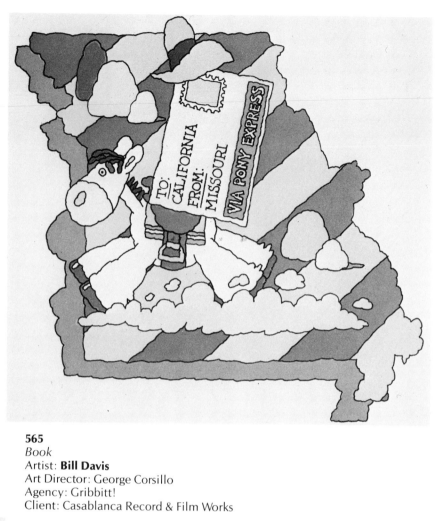

565
Book
Artist: **Bill Davis**
Art Director: George Corsillo
Agency: Gribbitt!
Client: Casablanca Record & Film Works

566
Institutional
Artist: **Ben Chase**
Art Director: Ben Chase
Client: Ben Chase

567
Institutional
Artist: **Ben Chase**
Art Director: Ben Chase
Client: Ben Chase

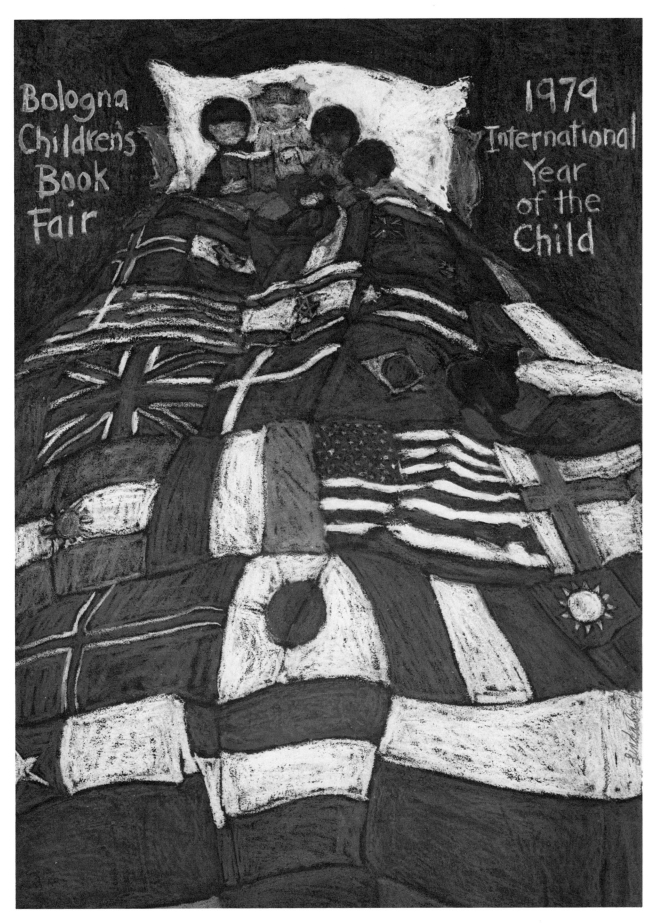

568
Advertising
Artist: **Linda Crockett-Hanzel**
Art Director: Linda Crockett-Hanzel
Client: Bologna Children's Book Fair

569
Institutional
Artist: **Michael David Brown**
Art Director: Ethel Kessler Freid
Agency: International Communication Agency
Client: United States Government

570
Book
Artist: **Elaine Raphael & Don Bolognese**
Art Director: Gordon Fisher
Title: The Scarlett Letter
Publisher: The Franklin Library

571
Advertising
Artist: **John Martin**
Art Director: David Wyman
Agency: Stephenson, Ramsay, O'Donnell Limited
Client: The Toronto International Film Festival

FOREIGN ILLUSTRATION/A SUPPLEMENT

572
Foreign
Artist: **John Martin**
Art Director: Rob Melbourne
Client: The City

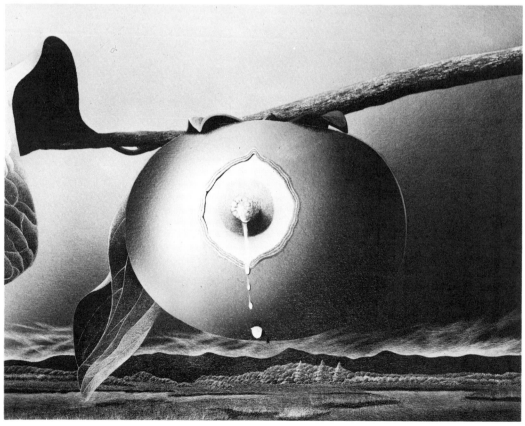

573
Foreign
Artist: **Yusuke Toda**
Art Director: Yusuke Toda
Client: Olympos Co., Ltd.

574
Foreign
Artist: **John Martin**
Art Directors: Mark Sarner/Eric Young
Client: Participaction

575
Foreign
Artist: **Shigeo Okamoto**
Art Director: Shigeo Okamoto
Agency: Shigeo Okamoto Design Center

576
Foreign
Artist: **Tom McNeely**
Art Director: Fred Levinski
Client: Fleetwood

577
Foreign
Artist: **Tom McNeely**

578
Foreign
Artist: **Tom McNeely**

579
Foreign
Artist: **Rei Ishikawa**
Art Director: Rei Ishikawa

580
Foreign
Artist: **Heather Cooper**
Art Director: Heather Cooper
Client: Jonathan James Books

581
Foreign
Artist: **Heather Cooper**
Art Director: Robert Burns
Client: Abitibi Provincal Papers

582
Foreign
Artist: **Maurice Kennel**
Art Director: Maurice Kennel

583
Foreign
Artist: **Maurice Kennel**
Art Director: Maurice Kennel

584
Foreign
Artist: **Maurice Kennel**
Art Director: Alfred Vetter
Client: Swissair

585
Foreign
Artist: **Jutaro Ito**
Art Director: Jutaro Ito
Title: Gulliver's Travels
Publisher: Kodansha Inc.

586
Foreign
Artist: **Jutaro Ito**
Art Director: Jutaro Ito
Title: Gulliver's Travels
Publisher: Kodansha Inc.

587
Foreign
Artist: **Jutaro Ito**
Art Director: Jutaro Ito
Title: Gulliver's Travels
Publisher: Kodansha Inc.

588
Foreign
Artist: **Toshio Komada**
Art Director: Toshio Komada
Client: Kamifusen Shop

589
Foreign
Artist: **Masao Minami**
Art Director: Masao Minami

590
Foreign
Artist: **Blair Drawson**
Art Director: Georges Haroutiun
Client: Homemakers' Magazine

591
Foreign
Artist: **Michael Turner**
Art Director: Paul Hoye
Client: Aramco World Magazine

592
Foreign
Artist: **Yoshikazu Nakata**
Art Director: Yoshikazu Nakata

46億歳の地球

広大な宇宙のかたすみに深かな恵まれた小惑星地球。地球にはわれわれ人類を生んでくれた。 しかし今、地球は老い始めている。この星をささえることができるのは、人間だけ。

593
Foreign
Artist: **Katsunori Usui**
Art Director: Katsunori Usui

594
Foreign
Artist: **Yoshimi Matsukawa**
Art Director: Yoshimi Matsukawa
Agency: ad-brain-center

595
Foreign
Artist: **Keiji Sugita**
Art Director: Keiji Sugita

596
Foreign
Artist: **Hidenobu Ito**
Art Director: Hidenobu Ito

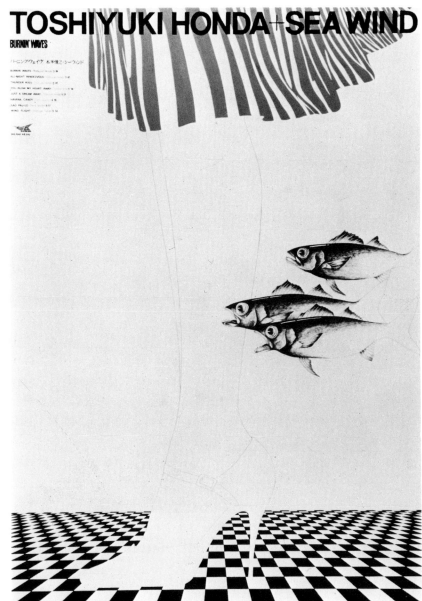

597
Foreign
Artist: **Shigeichi Umemura**
Art Director: Shigeichi Umemura
Agency: Design Studio Flush

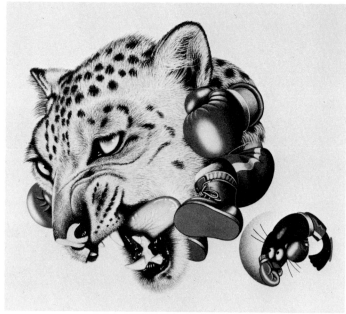

599
Foreign
Artist: **Atsushi Yoshioka**
Art Director: Toshiyasu Harada
Client: Asahi Sonorama Co., Ltd.

598
Foreign
Artist: **Atsushi Yoshioka**
Art Director: Toshiyasu Harada
Client: Asahi Sonorama Co., Ltd.

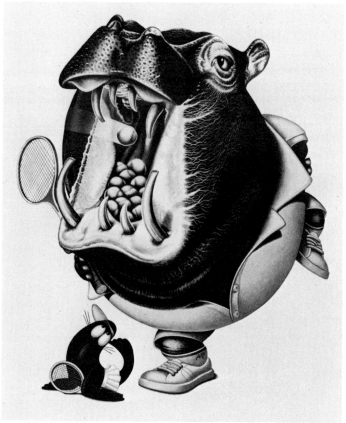

600
Foreign
Artist: **Heather Cooper**
Art Director: Alan Murphy
Client: Couples Club, Jamaica

601
Foreign
Artist: **Atsushi Yoshioka**
Art Director: Toshiyasu Harada
Client: Asahi Sonorama Co., Ltd.
Award of Excellence

602
Foreign
Artist: **Sadahito Mori**
Art Director: Kenichiro Fuzimoto
Agency: Hakuhodo Co., Ltd. Nagoya
Client: Nagoya Financing Bank

603
Foreign
Artist: **Sadahito Mori**
Art Director: Kenichiro Fuzimoto
Agency: Hakuhodo Co., Ltd. Nagoya
Client: Nagoya Financing Bank

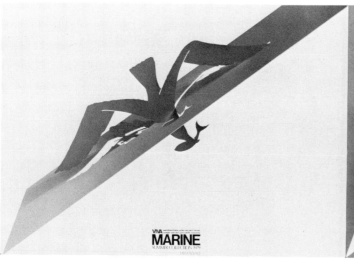

604
Foreign
Artist: **Ryosuke Matsuki**
Art Director: Ryosuke Matsuki
Agency: Graphic Space Neptune

605
Foreign
Artist: **Ryosuke Matsuki**
Art Director: Ryosuke Matsuki
Agency: Graphic Space Neptune

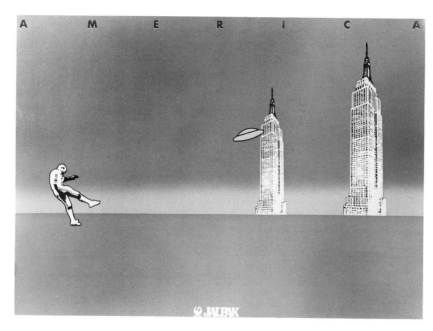

606
Foreign
Artist: **Yusaku Tomoeda**
Art Director: Yusaku Tomoeda
Agency: Tomoeda Yusaku Design House

607
Foreign
Artist: **Yoshiaki Hoshino**
Art Director: Yoshiaki Hoshino
Agency: Nambokusha Advertising Co., Ltd.
Client: Toyota Motor Sales Co., Ltd.

まごころ いっぱい
髙島屋のお歳暮　　髙島屋

608
Foreign
Artist: **Ikuo Takeda**
Art Director: Ikuo Takeda
Client: Takashimaya

609
Foreign
Artist: **Masayuki Miyata**
Art Director: Miss Syu Lei Ryu
Agency: Gabo Co., Ltd.
Client: Sâo Paulo Museum

610
Foreign
Artist: **Kazunori Miyamoto**
Art Director: Kazunori Miyamoto
Agency: Taiyo Package

611
Foreign
Artist: **Ikuo Takeda**
Art Director: Ikuo Takeda

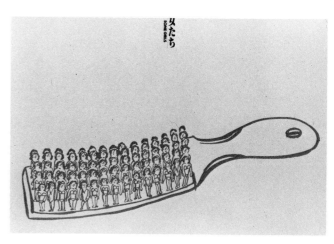

612
Foreign
Artist: **Ritsuo Kato**
Art Director: Yoshiro Kato

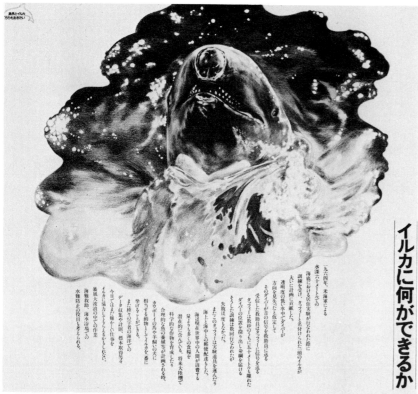

イルカに何ができるか

613
Foreign
Artist: **Mitsuhiro Okamoto**
Art Director: Mitsuhiro Okamoto

614
Foreign
Artist: **Sadahito Mori**
Art Director: Sadahito Mori
Agency: Mori Design Office

615
Foreign
Artist: **Kazuo Hakamada**
Art Director: Masayuki Yano
Client: Toshiba EMI

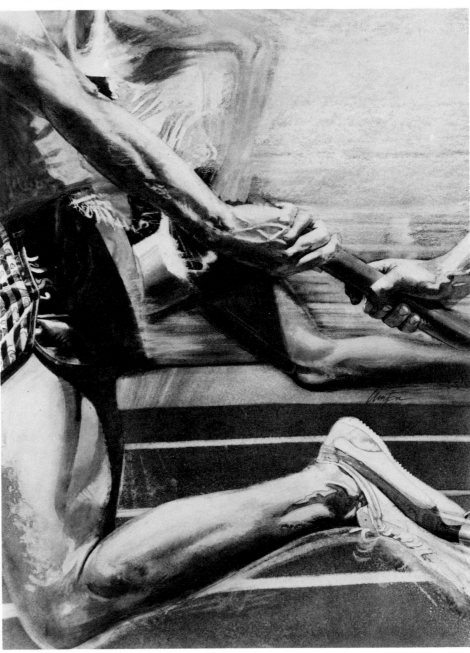

616
Foreign
Artist: **Brian Clinton**
Art Director: Arron Kamienko
Client: B.A.S.F.

618
Foreign
Artist: **Takuo Ohtakara**
Art Director: Takuo Ohtakara

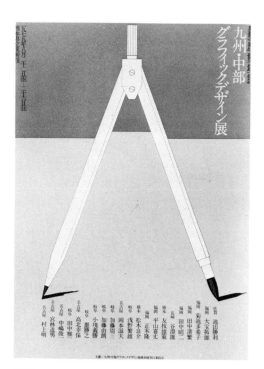

617
Foreign
Artist: **Yusaku Tomoeda**
Art Director: Yusaku Tomoeda
Client: Kyushu Chubu Graphic Design
　　　　Exhibition Committee

619
Foreign
Artist: **Masazumi Fujita**
Art Director: Masazumi Fujita
Client: Masazumi Fujita Design Office

621
Foreign
Artist: **Toshikane Tanaka**
Art Director: Toshikane Tanaka
Award of Excellence

620
Foreign
Artist: **Kazuo Hakamada**
Art Director: Kazuo Hakamada
Award of Excellence

622
Foreign
Artist: **Shun Ishikawa**
Art Director: Shun Ishikawa

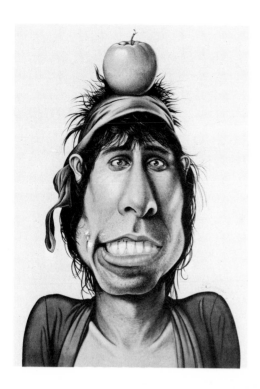

623
Foreign
Artist: **Saeko Tsuemura**
Art Director: Saeko Tsuemura

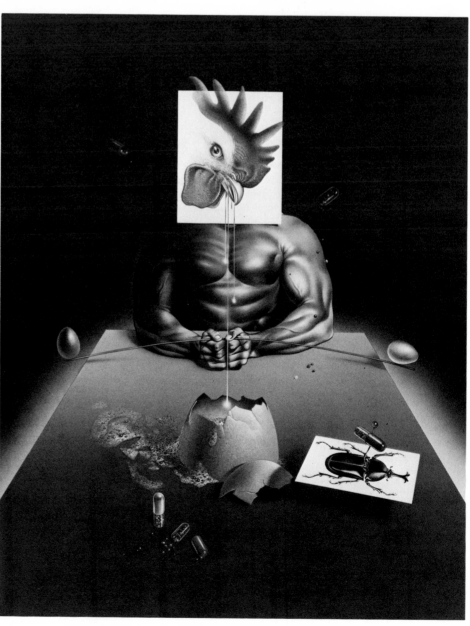

624
Foreign
Artist: **Shiro Nishiguchi**
Art Director: Shiro Nishiguchi

625
Foreign
Artist: **Lucinda Cowell**
Art Director: Francine Lawrence
Client: New English Library

NO,
MELT-DOWN

626
Foreign
Artist: **Noboru Matsuura**
Art Director: Noboru Matsuura

627
Foreign
Artist: **Etienne Delessert**
Art Director: Etienne Delessert
Client: Tournesol-Gallimard

628
Foreign
Artist: **Etienne Delessert**
Art Director: Etienne Delessert
Client: Supersaxo Film
Award of Excellence

629
Foreign
Artist: **Katsuhiko Ikeda**
Client: Sanrio Co. Ltd.

630
Foreign
Artist: **Blair Drawson**
Art Director: Georges Haroutin
Client: Homemakers' Magazine

631
Foreign
Artist: **Etienne Delessert**
Art Director: Etienne Delessert

632
Foreign
Artist: **Oswaldo Miranda**
Art Director: Oswaldo Miranda

633
Foreign
Artist: **Oswaldo Miranda**
Art Director: Oswaldo Miranda
Publication: Diario do Parana

ILLUSTRATORS 22 INDEX

ILLUSTRATORS

TITLES

ILLUSTRATORS 22 Production Credits

The type in this book is
Optima
Composition by
M.J. Baumwell, Typography
Offset plates and printing by
Connecticut Printers, Inc.
The paper is
Mead Black and White Dull
Paper Supplier
Andrews/Nelson/Whitehead Publishing Papers
Binding by
A. Horowitz and Son
Jacket printed by
Princeton Polychrome Press
Production supervision
Bill Hanashey, Hastings House

artists

Norman Adams, Robert Heindel,
Steve Karchin, Dick Krepel,
Rick McCollum, Fred Otnes,
Hodges Soileau

Represented by:
Bill Erlacher, Artists Associates
211 East 51 Street, New York, N.Y. 10022
Telephone: (212) 755-1365/6
Associate: Eileen McMahon

HEADS   by JARVIS

From the book, *A Pack of Dreams* © 1978 by Ann Greenwood.   Illustrations © 1978 by Bernard Colonna and Mary Elizabeth Gordon.   Published by Prentice-Hall, Inc., Englewood Cliffs, N.J. 07632.

Representing over forty illustrators
specializing in art for children of all ages.

Carol Bancroft, 185 Goodhill Road, Weston,
Connecticut 06883 (203) 226-7674.

"Let each become
all that he was created
capable of being."
—Thomas Carlyle

Work one-to-one
with six of
America's greatest
illustrators

Guest speakers
have included
Lorraine Allen,
Sam Antupit,
Darwin Bahm,
Walter Bernard,
Roger Black,
Herb Bleiweiss,
Dick Coyne,
John deCesare,
Etienne Delessert,
Harry O. Diamond,
Leo and Diane Dillon,
Bill Erlacher,
Dick Gangel,
Fritz Gottschalk,
Judeth Jampel,
Harvey Kahn,
Herb Lubalin,
Gerald McConnell,
David Merrill,
Susan E. Meyer,
Duane Michals,
Eugene Mihaesco,
Lou Myers,
Barbara Nessim,
Jack O'Grady,
Howard Paine,
Al Parker,
George Parker,
Art Paul,
Alan Peckolick,
Martin Pedersen,
Margery Peters,
Jerry Pinkney,
Don Ivan Punchatz,
Walt Reed,
Leslie Segal,
Maurice Sendak,
Neil Shakery,
Lou Silverstein,
Atha Tehon

Alan E. Cober,
Mark English,
Bernie Fuchs,
Bob Heindel,
Fred Otnes,
Robert Peak,
and their guests
at
**The Illustrators
Workshop.**

Photo: Duane Michals, Paris, France

For information
on future
programs write:
John deCesare,
Managing Director,
The Illustrators
Workshop, Inc.
47 Riverside Ave.
Westport, CT
06880

ARE YOU A POTENTIAL SUPERSTAR?

Isn't it about time you found out? Syracuse University's Independent Study Degree Program gives you an opportunity to work toward your MFA in Advertising Design or Illustration while you're working full time. And you study face-to-face with the top designers and illustrators in the industry.

For two weeks each summer (for three summers) you study with superstars like the former faculty listed below. The rest of the year you're working on independent study assignments and making a few long-weekend field trips to study with the top communicators right where they live and work. Places like New York,

Toronto, Chicago and London.

You'll find out more about how the pros work, you'll make more connections and you'll learn more than you can possibly imagine.

For information contact: Director, Syracuse University ISDP / **Room 45.** 610 E. Fayette Street / Syracuse, N.Y. 13202 / (315) 423-3269.

Study with the pros ALLAN BEAVER, JOE BOWLER, TOM CARNASE, MILTON CHARLES, STEVE COSMOPULOS, PAUL DAVIS, LOU DORFSMAN, GENE FEDERICO, DICK GANGEL, AMIL GARGANO, BOB GROSSMAN, DICK HARVEY, BOB HEINDEL, DOUG JOHNSON, DICK HESS, HELMUT KRONE, HERB LUBALIN, WILSON McCLEAN, JIM McMULLAN, JACQUI MORGAN, DAVE PASSALACQUA, ARTHUR PAUL, LARRY PLAPLER, SHIRLEY POLYKOFF, HEIDI RICKABAUGH, SAM SCALI, EILEEN HEDY SCHULTZ,.ISADORE SELTZER, BERT STEINHAUSER, MURRAY TINKELMAN, DON TROUSDELL & ROBERT WEAVER

Kirchoff/Wohlberg
Artists Representative

433 East 51 Street, New York, N.Y. 10022
212·753·5146
897 Boston Post Road, Madison, Ct. 06443
203·245·7308

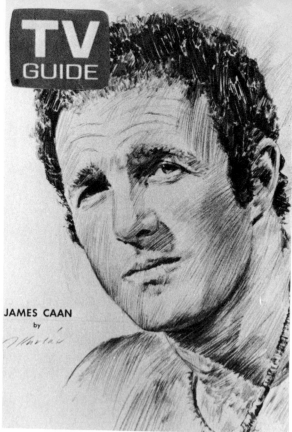

JAMES CAAN
by

Black & White Renderings by
artist: Raymond Kursar
One Lincoln Plaza-New York, N.Y. 10023
To view Portfolio call (212) 873-5605

See former ads in Illustrators Annuals 15,18,19,20,21.

AL PACINO

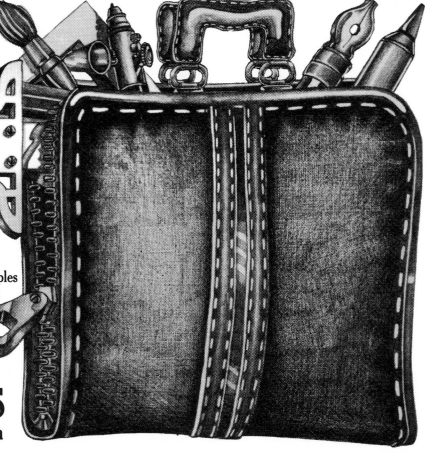